IT HAPPENED ON THE
MISSISSIPPI RIVER

James A. Crutchfield

gpp

Guilford, Connecticut

Text design by Nancy Freeborn
Map by M.A. Dubé © Morris Book Publishing, LLC

Library of Congress Cataloging-in-Publication Data is available on file.

ISBN 978-0-7627-4822-8

Front cover image: Mississippi River Fleet, U.S. gunboat *Brown,* circa 1861–1865, courtesy of the Library of Congress, LC-USZ62-62362
Back cover image: View of the St. Louis Bridge under construction, spanning the Mississippi River, circa 1881, courtesy of the Library of Congress, LC-USZ62-69757

Printed in the United States of America

10 9 8 7 6 5 4 3 2 1

CONTENTS

CONTENTS

PREFACE

From the Mississippi River's humble beginnings as a ten-foot-wide freshet running out of tiny Lake Itasca in northwestern Minnesota to its monumental rendezvous with the Gulf of Mexico a few miles beyond New Orleans, the mighty stream is probably the single most recognized geographical feature in North America. Separating East from West, the "Father of Waters" touches parts of ten states on its nearly 2,400-mile journey to the sea.

The historical vignettes found within these pages are representative of the long and varied history that surrounds the Mississippi, its valley, and its residents. From prehistoric Indian times at the magnificent native city of Cahokia, the thread of the past continues through the epic of George Rogers Clark's capture of Kaskaskia, General Ulysses S. Grant's first military victory at Belmont, the great steamboat race between the *Natchez* and the *Robert E. Lee,* and the story of America's pride of the inland waterways, the *Delta Queen.* Although this book can in no way be considered a complete history of the river, it is believed that the collection of varied and interesting stories contained herein will give the reader an excellent overview of the life and times of America's premier waterway.

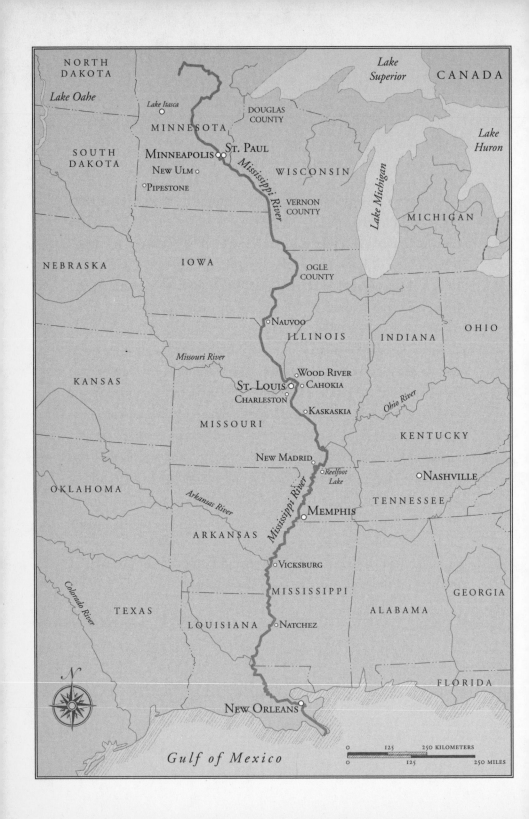

MISSISSIPPI RIVER

PREHISTORIC METROPOLIS
ON THE MISSISSIPPI

- A.D. 1000 -

Five hundred years before the first European explorers ever cast their eyes upon the magnificent beauty of the Mississippi River, prehistoric American Indians had already established a metropolis along the stream's eastern bank. Unexcelled in its architectural and cultural achievements, this was the empire of Cahokia, located in present-day central Illinois, just a stone's throw from St. Louis.

Cahokia was originally inhabited around A.D. 700 by a few Indians of the Woodland Culture tradition, but by the year 1000 it had grown to a city of nearly twenty thousand residents. By then, the cultural period known as the Mississippian had appeared, and the citizens of the four-thousand-acre town were well on their way to building the largest and most sophisticated Indian civilization north of the Rio Grande.

The Woodland founders of Cahokia were uncomplicated folk who made their living by farming the rich bottomlands along the

Mississippi River, fishing in the local streams, and hunting in the surrounding forests. Their homes were simple thatched huts, and they buried their dead in small, conical-shaped mounds. When Mississippian influences pushing north from Mexico began making themselves felt in the region, however, the peoples' lifestyles changed dramatically. By A.D. 900, the transition between Woodland and Mississippian cultures had been successfully completed, and Cahokia was well on its way to becoming the most heavily populated city in North America outside of Mexico.

By the time French explorers reached the area around Cahokia, the region was deserted, and local Indians had no recollection of the origins of the magnificent mounds that made up the once-populous town. More than one hundred platform and burial mounds were scattered across the countryside, the largest being the one that came to be called Monk's Mound. So named because French Trappist monks lived upon its terraces in the early 1800s, the huge structure measures 1,037 by 790 feet and stands 100 feet high. It covers sixteen acres and contains twenty-two million cubic feet of earth, all of it transported manually in baskets that probably held no more than two cubic feet each.

For years, scientists argued among themselves about who built the massive mounds at Cahokia and other sites scattered all over the eastern and middle sections of the United States. One school of thought suggested that a completely separate race of people, unrelated to the American Indians, was responsible. Opposing scholars, however, maintained that ancestors of the Indians had, indeed, performed the back-breaking construction and that, somehow, over the years, all memory of the event was lost to those Indians inhabiting the region when the first Europeans arrived.

In the late 1880s, Cyrus Thomas, an ethnologist for the Smithsonian Institution, solved the dilemma once and for all. Hundreds of temple and burial mounds across America were excavated, surveyed, and documented by Smithsonian archaeologists. At the end of the analysis period, Thomas—supported by tons of evidence—announced that American Indians were, indeed, responsible for the building of the mounds and that no mythical race of super humans was necessary to explain the phenomenon. In one of his many papers on the subject, Thomas wrote:

> *It is true that when we stand at the base of the great*
> *Cahokia mound and study its vast proportions, we can*
> *scarcely bring ourselves to believe it was built without*
> *some other means of collecting and conveying mate-*
> *rial than that possessed by the Indians. But what other*
> *means could a lost race have had? The Indians had*
> *wooden spades, baskets, skins of animals, wooden and*
> *clay vessels, and textile fabrics; they also had stone*
> *implements. Moreover, the fact should be borne in*
> *mind that this great mound is unique in respect to size,*
> *being more than treble in contents that of any other*
> *true mound in the United States. . . . As a general*
> *rule the labor necessary to build them could not have*
> *exceeded that which has often been performed by Indi-*
> *ans. It is also more than likely that all the people of a*
> *tribe, both men and women, aided in the work . . . .*

Over the years, Thomas's conclusion has been reconfirmed many times and, even today, it is the attitude held by most scientists.

Cahokia was not seriously re-examined until 1922 and, by then, several of the mounds and a great deal of the surrounding terrace work had been destroyed by farming practices. When professional archaeologists did begin work in the area, they unearthed a number of interesting features. One was a structure they called "Woodhenge," because of its similarity to Stonehenge, the mysterious Druid astronomical complex in England. They labeled another intriguing structure Mound 72.

Woodhenge was located a few hundred yards west of Monk's Mound and is believed to have served as a sort of solar calendar for Cahokia farmers who relied on the structure for seasonal planting and harvesting data. A large circle, consisting of forty-eight posts evenly set along the circumference, surrounded a center post that was used to align the rising or setting sun. Changing seasons and other agricultural events could thus be forecast by careful observation of the arrangements presented by the sun in relation to the various posts.

Mound 72, situated south of Monk's Mound, was a place of sacrifice. Archaeologists discovered the body of someone they assumed to be important, perhaps a king or high priest, reposed upon a blanket made of thousands of shell beads. Four male skeletons with heads and hands missing were found nearby, along with the bodies of fifty-three young women. The grisly evidence, supported by a large variety of grave offerings, strongly suggests that the men and women were slain at the time of the man's death in order to possibly accompany him to the afterlife.

Today, Cahokia is part of an Illinois State Historic Site that protects more than two thousand acres of the surrounding countryside, including the remains of the sixty-eight mounds that escaped the farmer's plow and urban sprawl. Designated as a World Heritage Site in 1982 by the United Nations, this fabulous city from the prehistoric past joins such shrines as the Taj Mahal, the Great Wall of China, the Egyptian pyramids, and the city of Rome in demonstrating the ingenuity of the human mind.

THE KENSINGTON STONE

- 1362 -

The bright, crisp November day in 1898 that Olaf Ohman chose to clear timber from part of his Douglas County, Minnesota, farm was much like most of the other days so far that autumn. Not yet winter, but with decided hints that cold temperatures were on the way, the weather was clear, beautiful, and just right for chopping down trees in preparation for opening new land to agriculture the following spring.

Ohman, his two sons, Olaf Jr. and Edward, along with a neighbor, Nils Flaaten, had spent most of the morning in the woodland when they happened upon an aspen tree needing to come down. After felling the trunk, the workers tried to pull out the rather extensive roots of what appeared to be a sixty- or seventy-year-old tree. As the men and boys alternatively dug into the ground with their spades, axes, and shovels, Ohman's tool hit a rock and came ricocheting back at him. Further exploration revealed a large rectangular stone, measuring about thirty-one inches long by sixteen inches wide and about six inches thick. As Ohman and his helpers finally disentangled the stone from the tree's intricate root system, they estimated that it probably weighed about two hundred pounds.

Not much attention was paid to the stone until near the end of the day, when Ohman and the others dragged their heavy load across the rugged ground and placed it in a pile with the other rocks and stones that their tiresome effort had uncovered. It was then, as he turned the stone over to expose its opposite side, that Ohman realized he was viewing something different from anything he had ever seen before.

Upon closer examination, the stone revealed ancient writing, a kind recognized by the Swedish-descended Ohman to be "runes." Casting his eyes over the rock, while carefully studying each of the scores of individually carved characters, Ohman remembered a book that he possessed, in which he had seen these same strange glyphs. When he got home that night, he located the volume, entitled *The Well-Informed Schoolmaster,* and compared the marks on his newly found stone with those pictured. To him and his family, the writing was identical.

According to O. J. Breda, a language professor at the University of Minnesota, the rock purportedly told of a group of Vikings who had become stranded in the neighborhood, but Breda was unable to translate the date of the incident. Assuming that the episode had something to do with the eleventh-century trans-Atlantic voyages of the Vikings, he promptly declared the stone and its carvings to be a fraud.

Ohman, nevertheless, proudly showed off his rock to neighbors in the nearby village of Kensington and even allowed it to be displayed in the window of the local bank. For several weeks, it drew the attention of the nation's press, and Ohman found himself to be somewhat of a celebrity. When other so-called scholars soon joined

Breda in denouncing the find as a fake, however, the dejected farmer took his stone home and dropped it in the barnyard where it lay for almost a decade.

In 1907, thirty-five-year-old Hjalmar Holand, a historian performing research into early Norwegian settlement patterns in Minnesota, heard about what by now was being referred to as the Kensington Stone and made a trip to see Olaf Ohman. The farmer took Holand to the barnyard, dug the stone out of the muck that had surrounded it for the last ten years, and presented it to him as a gift. The first task that the excited Holand undertook was a new translation of the runic writing on the face of the rock. According to him, the stone reads:

> [We are] 8 Goths (Swedes) and 22 Norwegians on
> [an] exploration-journey from Vinland through [round
> about] the West. We had camp by [a lake with] 2 sker-
> ries one day's-journey north from this stone We were
> [out] and fished one day After we came home [we]
> found 10 [of our] men red with blood and dead AV[e]
> M[aria] Save [us] from evil

Additional runes were lined along the narrow edge of the stone, and Holand translated them to read:

> [We] have 10 of (our party) by the sea to look after our
> ships (or ship) 14 days-journey from this island [in the]
> year [of our Lord] 1362

With this translation as the basis for additional research, Holand then turned his attentions to a study of original Scandinavian texts to determine if he could uncover evidence of a mid-fourteenth century, westward-bound exploration from Viking-land to America. He soon found proof that in 1354, King Magnus of Norway authorized a seaborne crusade that sent a number of mixed Scandinavians westward to Greenland with orders to re-Christianize the colony there. Sources indicated that the expedition, led by one Paul Knutson, did not return for eight years, plenty of time for its members to be blown off-course in the North Atlantic, to land on American shores near the mouth of the St. Lawrence River, and to wander up that stream and through the Great Lakes to present-day Minnesota.

Holand declared the Kensington Stone to be genuine and, as rapidly as his critics interjected a new doubt, he refuted them one by one. To those who believed that modern-day pranksters had created and planted the stone, Holand's response was simple, yet devastating. He later wrote:

> The stone was found gripped between the largest roots of a tree in such manner that it must have lain in its finding place at least as long as the tree had stood there . . . . This tree was about seventy years old. Seventy years anterior to 1898, when the stone was found, brings us back to 1828, which is more than twenty years before Minnesota was settled by white people and thirty-six years before the first Scandinavian reached Douglas County, where the stone was found. The earliest Scandinavian did not penetrate as far west as Chicago until 1834. If there were no Swedes or Norwegians in the Northwest at that early date (1828), the theory of a forgery is manifestly impossible.

Today, the debate over the controversial Kensington Stone continues. And it probably always will. One either believes or disbelieves its authenticity depending upon whether one subscribes to the belief that a European presence existed in North America *before* Columbus or not. To the disbelievers, the Kensington Stone is a fraud, along with all other artifacts that attempt to promote this theory. But, to those who do maintain that pre-Columbian contact existed, the Kensington Stone is proof positive that bands of Vikings, in addition to reaching the northeastern coast of the present-day United States, actually made their way hundreds of miles into the continent's interior. They point to the survivors of this group, and perhaps others, as the progenitors of the fair-skinned, blue-eyed Mandan tribe of Indians described by travelers up the Missouri River in the 1820s and 1830s.

EARLY EUROPEAN EXPLORATION ON THE MISSISSIPPI

- 1541–1681 -

Not much more than a quarter of a century passed between the time Christopher Columbus happened upon the West Indies in 1492, believing he had found a western route to India, and the beginning of his countrymen's systematic conquest and pillage of the New World. In 1519, Hernan Cortez and his Spanish army entered Mexico from Cuba and, over the next two years, beat the Aztec empire into submission. Thirteen years later, Francisco Pizarro and a handful of adventurer-soldiers defeated Peru's magnificent Inca kingdom in the same manner.

One of Pizarro's faithful lieutenants during the Spanish conquest of Peru was a young soldier named Hernando de Soto. According to a close associate, the Spaniard was:

> *an inflexible man, and dry of word, who, although*
> *he liked to know what the others all thought and had*

to say, after he once said a thing he did not like to be
opposed, and as he ever acted as he thought best, all
bent to his will.

De Soto was an early protégé of Vasco Nunez de Balboa, the discoverer of the Pacific Ocean. The youthful De Soto had spent considerable time adventuring in the New World, when his sovereign, Charles V, appointed him governor of Cuba, an area that extended to and included mainland Florida. In May 1539, De Soto and a small army of followers landed in present-day Tampa Bay, and immediately began making their way inland to survey his new domain.

For the next two years, the small group of Spanish brigands sloughed through the swamps of present-day Florida and southern Georgia, the high misty mountains of North Carolina and Tennessee, and the red clay flatlands of Alabama and Mississippi, before approaching the banks of the mighty Mississippi River near today's city of Memphis, Tennessee, sometime in May 1541. There, exclaimed one of the chroniclers of the journey, the river's width

> *. . . was near half a league over; a man standing on*
> *the shore could not be told, whether he were a man*
> *or something else, from the other side. The stream was*
> *swift, and very deep; the water, always flowing tur-*
> *bidly, brought along from above many trees and much*
> *timber, driven onward by its force. There were many*
> *fish of several sorts, the greater part differing from those*
> *of the fresh waters of Spain . . . .*

An encounter with menacing Indians in the neighborhood persuaded De Soto to build boats and navigate his men across the

Mississippi to the shores of present-day Arkansas. For the next twelve months, more wandering ensued, taking the small force almost to the Oklahoma border and back again to the Mississippi. There, upon the river's banks, De Soto died on May 21, 1542, almost three years to the day that his fleet landed in Florida and one year from the time that he supposedly became the first European to view the Mississippi River. His cloth-wrapped body was dropped into the stream somewhere as it flowed between present-day Arkansas and Mississippi.

Between De Soto's "discovery" of the Mississippi River in 1541, until 1673, when the Frenchmen, Louis Jolliet and Jacques Marquette, descended the stream for several hundred miles, the historical record is silent regarding European exploration. In the meantime, during that 132-year interim, much had changed among the American Indians who lived along the Mississippi River and its vast tributary system. De Soto's rude and ruthless entrance upon the scene had spelled doom to many tribal customs. Likewise, the disease that he and his men introduced, along with the results of his enslaving policy and warlike manner, sent the previously glorious "Mississippian" culture of mound-building Indians into extinction.

Thirty-six-year-old Marquette and twenty-eight-year-old Jolliet, the former a Jesuit missionary and the latter a fur trader from Quebec, departed from St. Ignace at the Straits of Michilimackinac on Lake Michigan, on May 17, 1673. After day upon day of canoeing and grueling portaging along the Fox and Wisconsin Rivers, the pair reached the Mississippi River one month later. As they entered the Mississippi, Father Marquette named the stream "Conception," and declared that he experienced " . . . a joy I cannot express."

Down and down the Mississippi the men rowed, sharing two birch-bark canoes with their companions. The leaders made many observations along the way, and when they came to the mouth of the Ohio River, Marquette reported on the condition of the Indian tribes that lived upriver. He wrote:

> *This river comes from the country on the east, inhab-*
> *ited by the people called Chaouanons (Shawanese), in*
> *such numbers that they reckon as many as twenty-three*
> *villages in one district, and fifteen in another, lying*
> *quite near each other; they are by no means warlike,*
> *and are the people the Iroquois go far to seek in order*
> *to wage an unprovoked war upon them; and, as these*
> *poor people cannot defend themselves (because they have*
> *no firearms), they allow themselves to be taken and car-*
> *ried off like sheep; and, innocent as they are, do not fail*
> *to experience at times the barbarity of the Iroquois who*
> *burn them cruelly.*

Marquette and Jolliet traveled down the Mississippi River as far as the mouth of the Arkansas River, where they turned around and began the long, laborious trip back upriver to their starting place. When they reached the mouth of the Illinois River, they ascended that stream and, by a series of portages, worked their way to Lake Michigan, where Jolliet prophesied a Lake Michigan–Mississippi River water connection that finally came true in 1900.

Nine years after Marquette and Jolliet made their monumental journey down the Mississippi River, one of their countrymen, Robert Cavalier de la Salle, repeated the trip and went one step further. In 1682, La Salle, whom the noted American historian, Francis Parkman, called " . . . without question, one of the most remarkable explorers whose names live in history," descended the Illinois River, entered the Mississippi, and traveled downstream all the way to the great river's mouth, reaching the Gulf of Mexico on April 9. Along the way, in the Tennessee country, the Frenchman built Fort Prudhomme, the first non-Indian structure ever built on Tennessee soil. Upon his arrival at the Gulf, La Salle declared the entire Mississippi River drainage area to be a possession of France and named the region, "Louisiana," in honor of his king, Louis XIV.

In years to come, ownership of the Mississippi River valley vacillated between Spain and France, predicated upon each country's claim to the territory as declared by its early explorers. The 1763 Treaty of Paris, which ended the French and Indian War in North America, gave much of the western portion of the valley to Spain, who in turn relinquished the region to France in 1800. In 1803, President Thomas Jefferson acquired the territory known as Louisiana for the United States, paying a total of $15 million for the 828,000-square-mile area.

THE FOUNDING OF NEW ORLEANS

- 1718 -

Antoine Simon Le Page Du Pratz, despite the French-sounding name, was born in Holland around 1695. After serving in the French army as a dragoon, or cavalryman, he migrated to Louisiana in 1718, the same year that the town of New Orleans was established. For the next sixteen years, he resided in the lowlands of Louisiana, spending eight of those years among the Natchez Indians of present-day Mississippi.

Twenty-four years after he returned to France, Du Pratz published a book entitled *The History of Louisiana*. The title was later translated from the French and published in London in 1774 as *The History of Louisiana, or of the Western Parts of Virginia and Carolina*. It is from Du Pratz's book, called by one authority "a tantalizing casket of historical treasure," that much of the early history of the lower Mississippi River is known.

New Orleans was still an idea in a city planner's mind when Du Pratz landed in Louisiana. Shortly afterward, the town began to take shape and was described by the writer as follows:

*New Orleans, the capital of the colony, is situated to
the East, on the banks of the Missisippi [sic], in 30
degrees of North Latitude. At my first arrival in Louisiana, it existed only in name; for on my landing I
understood M. de Biainviile, [Jean Baptiste, sieur de
Bienville] commandant general, was only gone to mark
out the spot; whence he returned three days after our
arrival at Isle Dauphine.*

Du Pratz reveals in his book that the logic for Bienville's site
selection was its proximity to Mobile, which was the primary settlement in the region, and its satisfaction of the requirement to accommodate large ships in its harbor. Even at this early date, the writer
must have foreseen the deadly repercussions that high water could
have on the desirable, but low-lying site, when he wrote,

*I should imagine, that if a town was at this day to be
built in this province, a rising ground would be pitched
upon, to avoid inundations; besides, the bottom should
be sufficiently firm, for bearing grand stone edifices
. . . . there are many habitations standing close
together; each making a causey [causeway, or levee] to
secure his ground from inundations, which fail not to
come every year with the spring: and at that time, if
any ships happen to be in the harbour of New Orleans,
they speedily set sail; because the prodigious quantity
of dead wood, or trees torn up by the roots, which the
river brings down, would lodge before the ship, and
break the stoutest cables.*

Apparently, sufficient quantities of limestone for Du Pratz's "grand stone edifices" had not yet been discovered in the region, causing the diarist to chide some of the town's leaders. He mused that some critics belittled the idea of using stone for building material since no stone was available. To these nay-sayers, he declared,

I might answer, and tell them, they have eyes, and see not. I narrowly considered the nature of this country, and found quarries in it; and if there were any in the colony I ought to find them, as my condition and profession of architect should have procured me the knowledge of them.

According to Du Pratz, the armory was located in the middle of town facing the Mississippi River and situated close to the parish church, "called St. Louis, where the Capuchins officiate, whose house is to the left of the church." To the right of the armory and church were the jail and guard-house. Nearby were the homes of the governor and the city's administrator, along with the magazine, or military warehouse. Along two sides of the complex were rows of barracks to house the troops. Common houses were for the most part built of brick with a few using brick and wood. The town's streets, making up sixty-six square blocks—eleven blocks along the river by six blocks deep—were laid out in grid fashion and crossed at right angles. Causeways fit for horse or coach travel lined the banks of both sides of the river.

Du Pratz went on to describe other French settlements in the region around the infant town of New Orleans, the primary one of which would become the city of Baton Rouge. Explaining how the settlement got its name, he wrote:

The Baton Rouge is also on the east side of the Mis-sisippi, and distant twenty-six leagues from New Orleans . . . . It is there we see the famous cypress-tree . . . . Some one of the first adventurers, who landed in this quarter, happened to say, that tree would make a fine walking-stick, and as cypress is a red wood, it was afterwards called le Baton Rouge. Its height could never be measured, it rises so out of sight.

During the nearly three hundred year existence of New Orleans, Mother Nature has not been kind, but the city and its people have survived, living and thriving under the flags of Spain, France, the Confederate States of America, and the United States. And, despite Hurricane Katrina's devastating effects, the city remains one of America's most exciting and vibrant communities, luring millions of tourists from all over the world.

THE NATCHEZ REVOLT

- 1729 -

Following La Salle's proclamation in 1682 that claimed the entire Mississippi River valley for France, European activities along the mighty stream were few. In 1699, Pierre le Moyne, sieur de d'Iberville, landed along the Gulf coast and reaffirmed La Salle's pronouncement of the ownership of the region for France. A little later, d'Iberville made contact with the Natchez tribe of Indians and, by 1713, his countrymen had established a trading post on the site of modern-day Natchez, Mississippi.

The French traders found the Natchez people to be extremely sophisticated and culturally advanced. They were a fairly small tribe, never numbering more than around five thousand individuals. In 1703, a French observer wrote that "this nation is composed of thirty villages, but the one we visited was the largest, because it contained the dwelling of the Great Chief, whom they call the Sun, which means noble." The village described was situated on the banks of present-day St. Catherine's Creek, just outside the city of Natchez.

The Grand Village of the Natchez consisted of several high earthen mounds surrounded by numerous living dwellings. Atop the mounds were the village's temples and houses for the chiefs. The walls of the houses of the common folk were built of wattle-and-daub construction, and the roofs were made of straw thatch. The region's normally warm winters made elaborate housing unnecessary, but the hot summers demanded insulation against the intense heat and humidity.

The Natchez tribe possessed the most highly advanced culture of any of the southeastern Indians, a culture which, no doubt, was a direct descendant of the Mississippian tradition that flourished over much of the South between A.D. 700 and A.D. 1500. Indeed, the Natchez enjoyed one of the most sophisticated civilizations north of the Aztec and Maya empires of Mexico and Central America. The people were accomplished farmers and skilled artisans and, like their Mississippian forebears, they were oriented toward great ceremonialism, maintaining the temple mound concept right down to the coming of the Europeans.

A class-conscious people, the Natchez were divided into four ranks: suns, nobles, honored people, and stinkards, or commoners. Strict rules were followed regarding intermarriage among the groups. The supreme chief, or Great Sun, held absolute power over his subjects and, upon his death, his wives were strangled and laid to rest with him for his afterlife pleasure.

Many of the customs and lifestyles of the Natchez were described in Antoine Le Page du Pratz's book referred to in the previous chapter. Du Pratz had lived among the tribe during the 1720s, and his keen observations have provided a great deal of information about this now-extinct people. Of Natchez clothing, du Pratz wrote:

During the hot season the men wear only a breechcloth. This is the skin of a deer dressed white or dyed black,

*but few except chiefs wear breechcloths of black skin
. . . . When it is cold the men cover themselves with a
shirt made of two dressed deerskins, which resembles
rather a nightgown than a shirt . . . . The women in
the warm season wear only an ell of Limbourg [cloth],
with which they cover themselves. They wind this
cloth about their bodies, and are well covered from the
belt to the knees . . . . With women as with men, the
remainder of the body is uncovered.*

The Natchez were ruthless adversaries in war, a fact that the French intruders learned all too soon. They were particularly harsh on captives. Du Pratz wrote that a typical prisoner was fed a final meal, then clubbed on the back of the head by the warrior who actually captured him. Then,

*. . . Having thus stunned him he [the warrior] cuts
the skin around his hair, puts his knees on his forehead,
takes his hair in both hands, pulls it from the skull,
and makes the death cry while removing the scalp in
the best manner he is able without tearing it.*

A long, agonizing death ritual followed, sometimes lasting for three days and nights, with the victim's body being slowly burned beyond recognition.

In 1716, three years after the first French traders arrived among the Natchez on St. Catherine's Creek, workmen built Fort Rosalie high on a bluff overlooking the Mississippi River, on the grounds of present-day Rosalie Mansion in downtown Natchez. The structure was named in honor of the Duchess of Pontchartrain and measured about 150 by 90 feet. Surrounded by palisades, the fort contained a guardhouse, barracks for the soldiers, and a powder magazine, but no corner bastions.

For the next few years, the presence of armed soldiers and a strong fortified post in their midst went a long way toward neutralizing any ill feelings that the Natchez might have had toward their French neighbors. But, by 1729, affairs between the two peoples had so badly deteriorated that conflict was inevitable. In November, shortly after the arrival of a new commandant at Fort Rosalie, affairs finally reached the breaking point.

Upon his assumption of command, one of the first acts that the naive newcomer ordered was the condemnation of the land upon which the Grand Village of the Natchez sat. To make matters worse, the reason he gave to the Indians for his callous demand was that he wanted to build his own French community on top of the site. When tribal authorities discussed the matter, they decided that the time had come to expel the bothersome Frenchmen once and for all.

On November 29, a strong force of Natchez tribesmen attacked the garrison at Fort Rosalie. When the smoke cleared, about 250 French soldiers had been killed and 300 women and children captured. So contemptuous of the arrogant new commander were the Natchez that they ordered a stinkard [commoner] to bludgeon the Frenchman to death so they did not dirty their hands. The fort and all of its buildings were burned to the ground.

When word of the massacre reached the French governor at New Orleans, he quickly organized an army and sent it north. The Indians holed up for a while in a hastily built fort of their own and, after being besieged for several days, finally sued for peace. Before the surrender terms could be consummated, however, the Natchez fled and eventually settled on the west side of the Mississippi near the mouth of the Red River. Here, some time afterward, the French army found and attacked them. The Indians capitulated, some of them fleeing to live in the villages of neighboring tribes and the rest being taken captive by the French. The Natchez as a people had been destroyed and, when the last of those few fugitives and prisoners died years later, the tribe became one of the earliest in North America to be classified extinct.

LACLÈDE AND THE BEGINNINGS
OF ST. LOUIS

- 1764 -

As the French and Indian War came to an end in favor of Great Britain, French authorities in North America correctly predicted that most of their holdings east of the Mississippi River would soon be turned over to the English victors. Kaskaskia, Vincennes, and Fort Chartres, along with several other settlements in the Illinois country, were officially surrendered as part of the Treaty of Paris signed in 1763.

Realizing that French influence in North America was a thing of the past, statesmen in Paris had already transferred Louisiana to France's ally, Spain, in November 1762, as part of the terms of the Treaty of Fontainebleau. The ceded territory stretched from the banks of the Mississippi River to the Rocky Mountains and from the Canadian border to the frontiers of New Spain. But news of the property transfer was slow getting to America from Europe, and by the time residents of the Illinois towns and forts looked for other, friendlier places in which to relocate, a Frenchman by the name of Laclède had already solved the problem.

Pierre de Laclède Liguest was born in the French Pyrenees around 1724, and in 1755 he migrated to New Orleans where he formed a partnership with Gilbert Antoine Maxent to trade with "savages of the Missouri," and other natives in the Mississippi River valley. He took a common-law wife, Marie Chouteau, who, along with her eight-year-old son, Auguste, became his devoted followers for the remainder of his life.

In the meantime, Maxent had been awarded an arrangement wherein he would have exclusive trading rights with the Indians along the west bank of the middle Mississippi River. In August 1763, he dispatched Laclède and young Chouteau, now a teenager, up the Mississippi to find a good site for the location of a trading post. After spending the winter at Fort Chartres on the Illinois side of the river, Chouteau and a small group of workers crossed to the west side in February 1764 and began work on the town that would become St. Louis, named after France's King Louis XV.

Several French Illinois residents pulled up stakes and resettled across the Mississippi in St. Louis, preferring the new French village to living under the rule of the victorious British. When news finally reached St. Louis that the entire Louisiana Territory in which it was located had been transferred to Spain two years earlier, forty to fifty families had already settled there, and the flavor, culture, and atmosphere of the village were entirely French, which they continued to be for many decades.

St. Louis grew steadily. About three years after its founding, a British army officer, Lieutenant Philip Pittman, traveled up the Mississippi River from New Orleans to survey His Majesty's newly acquired territories. Of the small village of St. Louis, he wrote:

This village is . . . on the west side of the Mississippi, being the present head quarters of the French in these parts . . . . The company has built a large house, and stores here, and there are about forty private houses and as many families. No fort or barracks are yet built. The French garrison consists of a captain-commandant, two lieutenants, a fort-major, one sergeant, one corporal, and twenty men.

By 1771, a total of 455 males, consisting of 415 French and 40 Negroes, called the village home. A quarter of a century later, according to Gilbert Imlay in his book, *A Topographical Description of the Western Territory of North America,* published in 1797, the town had grown to nearly one thousand residents. Imlay described St. Louis as:

. . . the most healthy and pleasurable situation of any known in this part of the country. Here the Spanish commandant and the principal Indian traders reside; who by conciliating the affections of the natives, have drawn all the Indian trade of the Missouri, part of that of the Mississippi (northwards) and of the tribes of Indians residing near the Wisconsin and Illinois rivers, to this village. In St. Louis are 120 houses, mostly built of stone. They are large and commodious. This village has 800 inhabitants, chiefly French; some of them have had a liberal education, are polite and hospitable. They have about 159 negroes, and large flocks of black cattle, etc.

One year later, Zenon Trudeau, the lieutenant-governor of Spanish Illinois, of which upper Louisiana was an administrative part, wrote in a letter to the governor that St. Louis "was the principal settlement of Illinois," and that it consisted of "948 persons of all ages and sexes."

By the turn of the nineteenth century, St. Louis found itself being settled by more and more Americans drifting across the Mississippi River. Spain soon relinquished control of all of Louisiana and ceded the vast territory back to France. In the meantime, Napoleon's dreams of world domination and his efforts at winning back his empire fell on hard times, compelling him to sell the entire region to the United States. President Thomas Jefferson quickly jumped at the opportunity to extend America's borders almost to the Pacific Ocean and authorized $15 million for Louisiana's purchase.

Jefferson commissioned Captains Meriwether Lewis and William Clark to explore the new territory and, in the spring of 1804, the pair, along with forty or so companions, left St. Louis for the long trek to the Pacific and back again. It was the information brought back by the Lewis and Clark Expedition that excited some entrepreneurial Americans about the fortunes in furs that might be made west of the Mississippi. For the next half-century, St. Louis became the headquarters and primary depository for the western American fur trade and at one time was the home to several major fur companies. One of the earliest and most important outfits, the Missouri Company, was organized in 1794 by the same Auguste Chouteau who, as a youngster, helped found the town.

THE FALL OF KASKASKIA

- 1778 -

During late June 1778, American colonists and British redcoats were fighting it out in Monmouth, New Jersey, in what was to be the last great battle of the Revolutionary War in the north. At the same time, far to the west on the banks of the Mississippi River, another equally dramatic event was unfolding. There, Virginia-born, Kentucky-bred Lieutenant-Colonel George Rogers Clark gathered his small army of volunteers in preparation for an attack on the British-held, but primarily French-occupied, stronghold at Kaskaskia, located deep in the Illinois country.

For several years, the British had maintained a string of posts in the wilderness country situated between the Great Lakes in the north and the Ohio River in the south. Among the forts were those at Detroit, Kaskaskia, Vincennes, and Cahokia. With the onset of the Revolution, several of the Indian tribes that occupied the region had allied themselves with Great Britain, on the assumption that His Majesty's well-disciplined armies would quickly annihilate the ragtag militia that the colonies had been able to raise. Then, the natives thought, with the upstart, always land-hungry American settlers out of the way, old relationships with the British could be re-established and affairs could revert to normal.

The British commander at Detroit was Henry Hamilton, a career soldier who possessed a particular hatred for the infant United States. He soon became known to friend and foe alike as "The Hair Buyer," because of his policy of paying bounties on American scalps. Indians from around the region found a steadfast friend in Hamilton, and they were eager to accommodate his lust for American hair, in return for which he rewarded them with rifles, ammunition, and other badly needed supplies.

As the Revolution got underway in earnest, George Rogers Clark became particularly worried about the fate of his neighbors in Kentucky. In late 1776, the entire region presently known by that name was still part of the Virginia colony and organized into a separate county. Thousands of emigrants flocked from their homes in the Allegheny Mountains to settle the rich lands in the central portion of the future commonwealth. Responding to the incursion, several Indian tribes, including the powerful Shawnees, soon began drenching the Kentucky frontier in blood.

Clark correctly suspected that British authorities in Detroit, including Hamilton himself, were actively fueling the Indians' anger over the alarming encroachment upon their lands. As the twenty-five-year-old Kentuckian watched conditions on the frontier rapidly deteriorate and, as he came to realize that the struggling and overworked American army in the east could not be called upon for protection, he decided to take matters into his own hands.

Clark's plan was simple. He would assemble several companies of volunteers from Kentucky and surrounding areas and march on the British garrisons at Kaskaskia, Illinois, and Vincennes,

Indiana. According to Clark, the American occupation of the two outposts:

> *would distress the garrisons at Detroit; it would fling*
> *the command of the two great rivers [the Mississippi*
> *and the Ohio] into our hands, which would enable us*
> *to get supplies of goods from the Spaniards and carry on*
> *trade with the Indians.*

With this scheme in mind, Clark proceeded at once to Williamsburg, where he and his ideas for occupying the far-flung British forts were well received by Virginia's governor, Patrick Henry, as well as by Henry's advisors, Thomas Jefferson, George Mason, and George Wythe. Governor Henry gave Clark his marching orders in early January 1778.

When Clark left his little army's mustering ground near today's Louisville, Kentucky, on June 24, 1778, bound for Kaskaskia, he was accompanied by only 175 men, far fewer than he had hoped to recruit. But, manpower was scarce, since most able-bodied individuals were already committed to fighting in the East. Undaunted, Clark and his followers sped down the Ohio River aboard several flatboats until they reached Fort Massac, situated on the north bank of the stream, near the mouth of the Tennessee River. From there, they marched overland to Kaskaskia where they arrived during the evening of July 4.

Clark and his small command caught the British napping at Kaskaskia and took the outpost without firing a shot. The French inhabitants of the town were apprised of the fact that France had only recently taken the side of the United States in the war with Great Britain and most of them welcomed the Americans with open arms. Several days later, small contingents of Americans were dispatched to Cahokia and Vincennes and peacefully captured those two posts as well. Clark then met with the leaders of the major Indian tribes that inhabited the region—the Kaskaskia, Peoria, Chippewa, Ottawa, Potawatomi, Miami, Sac, Fox, and Winnebago—and persuaded most of them to switch their loyalties from the British to the United States. The powerful Shawnees were noticeably absent from the negotiations.

In the meantime, Lieutenant-Governor Hamilton in Detroit, smarting over Clark's bold and successful foray into British-held territory, vowed to strike back. He raised a small force of thirty-five soldiers, sixty friendly Indians, and seventy-eight French allies, and marched on Fort Sackville, the post at Vincennes, picking up a few hundred more Indians along the way. The weak American and French garrison at the fort provided little resistance for Hamilton and was forced to surrender in mid-December 1778.

In early February 1779, Clark took the offensive again. He left Kaskaskia with several companies of men, bound for Vincennes. They marched for days, much of the time through ankle-deep mud and chest-level floodwaters left by the swollen Wabash, Little Wabash, and Fox Rivers. When the Americans finally arrived at the outskirts of Vincennes on February 23, they were exhausted, wet, hungry, and ready for a fight.

Although Hamilton had improved Fort Sackville and added blockhouses at the corners, thereby making the structure practically impregnable for foot-soldiers, the lieutenant-governor labored under the false impression that Clark's command consisted of hundreds of men. Since his own garrison was primarily defended by only a few British redcoats, Hamilton chose to surrender the installation and himself to Clark's jubilant men after only a few hours of desultory resistance.

George Rogers Clark's assorted victories over Lieutenant-Governor Hamilton's chain of outposts in the Mississippi River valley during 1778 and 1779 went a long way toward neutralizing British influence among the various Indian tribes of the area during the remainder of the Revolution. And, in the final analysis, they guaranteed American settlement in the valuable region that less than a decade later became the Northwest Territory.

LEWIS AND CLARK AT WOOD RIVER

- 1803 -

Most American history books declare that the Lewis and Clark Expedition got underway on May 14, 1804, when captains Meriwether Lewis and William Clark and forty or so men departed St. Louis to explore the vast, newly acquired Louisiana Territory. Over the next twenty-eight months, the monumental "voyage of discovery," as the mission was sometimes called, eventually carried the adventurers through eight thousand miles of virtually unexplored wilderness to the Pacific Ocean and back again. The journey concluded years of dreaming and planning on the part of Thomas Jefferson, whose penchant for scientific matters drove him to organize the expedition in the first place.

Actually, however, the expedition had its real origin on January 18, 1803. On that day, President Jefferson requested and received from Congress an appropriation of $2,500 to fund a research junket to the Pacific Ocean, ostensibly to identify commercial opportunities that could be derived by establishing trade with the trans-Mississippi

Indian tribes. According to Jefferson, "an intelligent officer with ten or twelve chosen men . . . might explore . . . even to the Western ocean, have conferences with the natives on the subject of commercial intercourse . . . and return with the information acquired in the course of two summers."

Less than three months after Jefferson convinced Congress to finance what eventually became the Lewis and Clark Expedition, the United States government, under his direction, purchased the Louisiana Territory from France. Reaching from the Mississippi River to the crest of the Rocky Mountains and from the Canadian border to the Gulf of Mexico, the huge area encompassed 828,000 square miles. For about three cents an acre, Jefferson overnight doubled the size of the United States.

But Jefferson had not waited for the purchase to become final before he authorized Lewis and Clark to work out the logistics of the soon-to-begin monumental journey. In a letter to Lewis dated November 16, 1803, a full month before the Louisiana Purchase became legal, Jefferson gave Lewis his marching orders. The president told him that "The object of your mission is single, the direct water communication from sea to sea formed by the bed of the Missouri and perhaps the Oregon."

Between the time Jefferson received the necessary funds to pay for the expedition and December 1803, Lewis spent most of his time in Philadelphia, Washington, D.C., Harper's Ferry, and Pittsburgh buying supplies and equipment for the journey, conferring with Jefferson, and having the boats built. Clark, in the meantime, busied himself with recruiting the men who would be needed for the transcontinental trek.

By late 1803, Lewis and Clark had rendezvoused along the lower Ohio River and made plans for the entire command to move up the Mississippi River toward St. Louis. However, since

Spain had only retroceded Louisiana to France shortly before the American purchase of the territory, Spanish officials still governed St. Louis. When they communicated to Lewis that they preferred his expedition crew stay on the American side of the Mississippi, a winter camp site was selected at the mouth of the Wood River, or the Dubois as the French called it, located about eighteen miles upstream from St. Louis and across the Mississippi from the mouth of the Missouri.

In mid-December 1803, the few settlers who lived along the Illinois side of the Mississippi River watched in amazement as the assemblage of one keelboat and two pirogues (canoes) carrying almost half a hundred men and one dog hugged the east bank and progressed slowly upstream. Some of the strangers were dressed in military attire signifying that they were members of the United States army, but others wore simple buckskin or homespun woolen clothes that were common in this part of the frontier at the time. When the tiny flotilla reached the mouth of the Wood River, the men clambered ashore and immediately started work on the camp in which they would spend the winter.

When they had completed building the several log cabins in the makeshift settlement that would later be called Camp Dubois, expedition members unloaded their cargo from the boats and prepared for the coming cold weather. The site of the camp was a pleasant enough place. Clark, in his normal, less-than-perfect, English, described it as:

> . . . *butifull beyond discription; a rich bottom well timbered, from one to three mile wide, from the river to a Prarie; which runs nearly parrilal to the river from about three miles above me, to Kaskaskia and is from*

three to 7 miles wide, with gradual rises and several
streams of running water, and good Mill seats . . . .

The five months that the men of the Lewis and Clark Expedition spent at Camp Dubois were rather uneventful. Lewis and Clark
alternated their personal bases of operations between St. Louis and
the camp. The winter turned out to be very cold, with temperatures
plummeting on several occasions to well below zero. The Mississippi's waters froze over along the riverbank, and the men could see
the ice flows coming out of the mouth of the Missouri. To protect
them from damage, the boats were pulled ashore and docked on high
ground.

In the meantime, the men occupied their time with target practice, drilling, hunting, preparing for the long journey that would
formally begin the following May, and on more than one occasion,
fighting among themselves. Several courts-martial were held, with
the usual punishment to the guilty being a sound flogging.

Finally, May 14, 1804, the day all of the men had been waiting
for, arrived. Now, the expedition would get started in earnest. The
keelboat and the two pirogues were carefully loaded, while the men
double-checked their personal supply list. It was late in the day when
all of the final preparations were made but, when everything was in
order, the three craft labored across the swift current of the Mississippi River into the mouth of the Missouri. Captain Clark was in
command since Lewis had traveled ahead and was to meet the main
party at St. Charles, located just a few miles up the Missouri. Of the
momentous occasion, Clark wrote in his journal:

Set out from Camp River a Dubois at 4 oClock p.m.
and proceeded up the Missouris under Sail to the first
Island in the Missouri and Camped on the upper point

opposit a Creek on the South Side below a ledge of
limestone rock, Called Colewater, made 4½ miles . . . .

Although Clark commented that it was a cloudy, windy, rainy day, he reported that the men were "in high Spirits."

After rendezvousing with Lewis at St. Charles, the entire flotilla started its long, laborious journey up the Missouri. It would be more than two years before the men passed this way again.

THE TRANSFER OF LOUISIANA

- 1804 -

It is doubtful that more than a handful of those assembled—a mixture of the town's original settlers from Illinois, French fur trappers and traders, and not a few Indian visitors—were totally aware of the complex diplomatic issues that had brought them together this day. It was March 9, 1804, and the three hundred or so spectators had slowly gathered in front of St. Louis's Government House, perched high on a bluff overlooking the broad Mississippi River.

For the past several weeks, plans had been made for the transfer of Upper Louisiana to American ownership. Now the time had finally come to officially execute the transfer, and the affair promised to be one of much pomp and gaiety. Here, on the remote western frontier, any kind of festivity was appreciated and, as the minutes passed quickly, the crowd grew more and more restless. Finally, Captain Amos Stoddard, a handsome, young, American army officer, stepped forward.

Stoddard, the commander of a company of infantry assigned to Fort Kaskaskia across the river, was one of the few present who had some knowledge of the behind-the-scenes maneuvering that had taken place over the past year and would culminate in the ceremonies about to take place. The captain realized the vast land known as Louisiana had originally belonged to the French by virtue of La Salle's claim in 1682. He also knew that at the end of the French and Indian War, France had ceded Louisiana to her ally, Spain, who claimed it until 1800, when that country retroceded, or returned, the same land to France. Napoleon, eyeing a world dominated by France, had high hopes for Louisiana until his army began losing thousands of men and millions of francs annually in Santo Domingo while trying to crush a slave revolt.

In order to protect American shipping down the Mississippi River and through the port of New Orleans, President Thomas Jefferson had sent a delegation, headed by Robert Livingston, to Paris in 1801 with a view in mind to purchase from the French the Island of New Orleans, as well as East and West Florida. Negotiations had dragged on as Napoleon became more and more frustrated by his army's continued loss of manpower, matériel, and money in the West Indies. As more time passed, Napoleon began considering the sale of *all* of Louisiana to the United States. In a series of meetings called to discuss such a possibility, one of his trusted advisors exclaimed:

> *We should not hesitate to give up Louisiana which is about to slip away from us anyhow. War with England is inevitable. Shall we be able with very inferior naval forces to defend the province against that power? This conquest would be still easier to the Americans. The province is scarcely inhabited. You have not fifty soldiers there. Where are your means of sending garrisons*

*thither? Can we restore fortifications that are in ruins,
and construct a long chain of forts upon a frontier of
four hundred leagues?*

Convinced that Louisiana was a losing proposition to his country, Napoleon decided to offer the whole of the territory, including New Orleans—more than half a billion acres—to the Americans. Robert Livingston and James Monroe, who had traveled to Paris to assist in the negotiations, agreed to the proposal and a price of $15 million. A treaty to that effect was drawn up on April 30, 1803, and signed by the interested parties two days later. And thus, Louisiana—whose boundaries were imprecise, but which was thought to extend from the Mississippi River to the crest of the Rocky Mountains and from New Spain to Canada—was acquired by the United States.

Captain Stoddard, in anticipation of the historic moment that was soon to take place, arrived in St. Louis in late February to prepare for the occasion. He had only recently received the news from French authorities that since Spain had never officially returned the territory to France under the earlier treaty terms—and in the absence of an official representative from Paris—he had been chosen to represent Napoleon and to receive the ownership of Louisiana for France from the Spanish lieutenant-governor in St. Louis.

President Jefferson, in the meantime, had also directed Stoddard to represent his administration at the proceedings and to accept the territory as it passed from France to the United States. Stoddard's friend, Meriwether Lewis, who had been assigned by Jefferson to lead the exploration party to the Pacific Ocean and back, had accompanied him, but pressing business at the expedition's winter camp on the Illinois side of the Mississippi had temporarily called him back. Now, a few days later, Lewis had returned to St. Louis to assist Stoddard in the details of the transfer.

When the time for the proceedings arrived, Stoddard, the Spanish lieutenant-governor, and other officials approached the Government House. As the men stepped onto the porch, the Spaniard faced the crowd and read a proclamation advising the town's residents that the territory was being relinquished by Spain. Spanish soldiers saluted with their rifles and Spanish cannons positioned on a nearby hillside boomed. The Spanish flag was lowered from the staff and replaced by the French tricolor. Stoddard accepted the transfer papers in the name of France.

On the following day, a similar ceremony took place, only this time, American army troops replaced the Spanish soldiers, and Captain Stoddard found himself in the odd position of handing over the Louisiana Territory, as a French delegate, to himself, as the American representative. The French tricolor was lowered and the Stars and Stripes banner of the United States was raised above the Government House.

The crowd slowly dismissed. Some of the people were happy, some were sad. Although Louisiana had been under Spanish rule for the past forty years, French influence had always dominated the region. Naturally, there was much apprehension among the territory's officials about the new allegiance the people would have to the United States. An obscure spectator to the ceremony, Black Hawk, a chief of the Sauk and Fox tribe, was not too sure of what life with the Americans might bring. He anticipated the future when he declared, "We had always heard bad accounts of the Americans from Indians who had lived near them and we were sorry to lose our Spanish Father, who had always treated us with great friendship." Before too many more years, Black Hawk would be heard from again and, when he was, it was not good news for his American neighbors.

"KAINTUCKS" ON THE MISSISSIPPI

- 1807 -

Integrally woven into the rich historical tapestry of the lower Mississippi River valley is the story of the Natchez Trace. Stretching for 450 wilderness miles between Natchez, Mississippi, in the south and Nashville, Tennessee, in the north, the trail is one of the oldest roadways in the entire country which, at one time or another, served wild animal herds, prehistoric and historic tribes of Indians, farmers and merchants, the U.S. Post Office, and the American military establishment.

Between the late 1780s and 1811, the old Trace was called the "Path to the Choctaw Nation" along its southern route and the "Chickasaw Trace" throughout its northern portion. Later, when it was a widely used thoroughfare for Kentucky and Tennessee boatmen returning home from Natchez and for post riders who frequented it to deliver the U.S. mail between Natchez and Nashville, it became known as the "Road from Nashville in the State of Tennessee to the Grindstone Ford of the Bayou Pierre in the Mississippi Territory." It was not until around 1820, ironically almost a decade after its primary commercial use had subsided, that the name "Natchez Trace" was bestowed upon it.

After Central Kentucky and Middle Tennessee were claimed by farmers and merchants from the Appalachian Mountain region during the 1770s and 1780s, it was only a matter of time until the fledgling settlements had grown sufficiently in number and population to require a practical outlet for the produce of their farms and manufactories. A sizeable commerce developed quickly, and the volume of shipments increased yearly until by 1790, sixty-four boatloads of goods from Tennessee and Kentucky were processed at the markets in Natchez.

New Orleans and Natchez were natural markets for the over-mountain settlers of Tennessee and Kentucky to select for the disposition of their goods. The only method of transporting wares to an alternative market back east was the overland route through hundreds of miles of untamed wilderness, or else overland as far as the Ohio River and then upriver to Pittsburgh and beyond. Neither of these choices was a good one, and each implied extensive planning, considerable time, and an abundance of labor.

On the other hand, in order to move goods to Natchez or to New Orleans, all the farmer-merchant had to do was to build a flat-boat, load it with his produce, and float it down the inland waterway system—the Ohio and Mississippi Rivers, and in the case of the Nash-villians, the Cumberland—to market. Once there, after the goods had been sold, the flatboat was broken up and sold for lumber, permitting the owner and his crew to walk back home along the old Indian trail which would later become known as the Natchez Trace.

These simple business transactions by Tennessee and Kentucky backwoodsmen were responsible for the genesis of an entire era of life and lore along the Natchez Trace and the lower Mississippi River valley. The period has become known as the Boatmen's Era, because during its brief life from the early and middle 1780s to around 1811, hundreds of farmers-turned-boatmen shipped millions of pounds of farm produce and home industry products down the Mississippi, sold their goods, collected their money, and made their way back up the Natchez Trace to Nashville and to their respective homes.

To the people along the lower Mississippi River, the flatboat men eventually came to be known as Kaintucks, whether or not they hailed from Kentucky. Even though the Kaintucks started out as farmers-turned-boatmen, in time a professional class of flatboat men evolved, who made it their business to haul goods downstream to Natchez and New Orleans. A contemporary observer was less than kind in his remarks of the group as a whole. According to him, the Kaintucks were:

> . . . *dirty as Hottentots, their dress a shirt and trousers of canvass, black, greasy, and sometimes in tatters, the skin burnt wherever exposed to the sun, each with a budget, wrapt [sic] up in an old blanket, their beards eighteen days old, added to the singularity of their appearance, which was altogether savage.*

Since the Kaintucks necessarily lived aboard their crafts for weeks at a time, some of the more elaborate flatboats were fitted out with sleeping quarters and a fireplace that was used for cooking and for providing heat in cold weather. But none of the boats were so valuable that they could not be broken up into lumber at their destination, and for good reason. It took thirty men a total of three months to row and pole a flatboat from New Orleans to Cairo, in the Illinois country. On the other hand, walking the Trace to Nashville and then to travel one of the northern roads out of that town to the same destination required less than half the time and was much easier.

The time of the Boatmen's Era in Natchez Trace history overlapped to a degree that of the next period when the United States aspired to convert the old thoroughfare into a national road. At the turn of the eighteenth century, while the government was laying plans for the acquisition of the property from the Indians and making decisions for the improvement of the Natchez Trace, the road was still used day in and day out by Kaintucks and others just as it had been all through the 1780s and 1790s. In fact, the boatmen used the trail for several years after the improvements were made, since it was still the only practical way to get to Tennessee, Kentucky, and points beyond from Natchez and New Orleans. Not until the advent and proliferation of the steamboat were the commercial uses of the Natchez Trace replaced by the more universal ones of mail service, transportation of military troops, and private travel in general.

In 1801, after a few months of attempting to use the Natchez Trace as a mail route between Nashville and Natchez, the postmaster-general of the United States wrote to the secretary of war suggesting that army troops be used to improve the horrible conditions along the way. Accordingly, over the next couple of years, more than one-half of the roadway's length was widened, cleared of trees, and provided with bridges over creeks. Concerned about bandits along the Trace's length, Tennessee's governor requested army assistance in protecting travelers. President Thomas Jefferson responded by offering "a reward of four hundred dollars to any Citizen or Indian who shall apprehand [sic] one of more of the Banditti who have been guilty of attacking, robing [sic] & murdering persons on the road to the Indian Country between Nashville and Natchez . . . . "

Over the next few years, the Trace was used primarily as a post road, as well as a convenient way to move troops to the Gulf Coast when the War of 1812 became imminent. Andrew Jackson used it frequently and, in October 1809, Meriwether Lewis, of Lewis and Clark Expedition fame, lost his life along the trail at a small inn located in Tennessee, just south of Nashville.

Today, the popular Natchez Trace Parkway, a unit within the National Park Service, winds its way along the general route of the old Natchez Trace. Gliding along the Trace in air-conditioned comfort, the modern tourist has little empathy or understanding of the dangers that once lurked in the dark forests, ever ready to confront the weary traveler of yesteryear.

THE NEW MADRID EARTHQUAKE

- 1811–1812 -

With seemingly increasing frequency, violent earthquakes—some far away and some nearby—lash their fury upon the earth and its inhabitants. Actually, however, earthquakes—at least the small ones—are not uncommon; in a year's time several hundred quakes might rattle the planet's surface, and all but a few of them go relatively unnoticed.

In North America, whenever earthquakes are mentioned, attentions usually turn to the Pacific coastline, the long strip of volcanically active land that stretches from Alaska to Mexico. The disastrous quake on Good Friday 1964, in Alaska, the 1985 cataclysm in Mexico City, and two more recent ones in California all remind us that Nature's fury is at its highest level when rock layers, embedded deep within the earth's interior, relentlessly pull at each other.

As geologically active as the West Coast is, however, many modern-day scientists believe that the worst earthquakes ever to hit North America occurred in the Mississippi River valley in an area lying in western Tennessee and eastern Missouri. Because the region was largely uninhabited at the time—late 1811 and early 1812—a real judgment of the killer quakes' severity is difficult to determine at this late date. Considering the geologic evidence, however—the fault line, the creation of Reelfoot Lake, and other remains—it is believed that the New Madrid earthquakes, as they have become known in history, surpassed even the San Francisco rumblings of 1906.

The worst of the nearly nineteen hundred shock waves that emanated from the New Madrid quakes during the three-month period between the first tremor and the following March 14 were felt all over the eastern United States, from Quebec in the north to New Orleans in the south. Church bells in Charleston, South Carolina, were set to ringing, while in Washington, D.C., chandeliers and windows in homes throughout the area rattled furiously. In Nashville, Tennessee, some one hundred miles to the east, the tremors were so severe that construction workers on a structure being built on the Public Square left the job for fear of being knocked off the roof.

John Haywood, an eminent jurist and prolific historical writer who is sometimes called the "father" of Tennessee history, described the New Madrid quakes in his 1823 book, *Natural and Aboriginal History of Tennessee.*

> *The earthquakes of 1811 commenced on the 16th of December, half-past two o'clock in the morning; and have been felt at intervals up to 1819, and as late as July 1822. The first shocks, which were the most violent, had these effects. The water in the Mississippi near New Madrid rose in a few minutes twelve or fourteen feet, and fell like a tide. Some lakes were elevated, and*

the bottom raised above the common surface of the
earth in the neighborhood, and still remains so . . . .

The motions in Tennessee were sometimes, but seldom, perpendicular; resembling a house raised, and suddenly let fall to the ground. Explosions like the discharge of a cannon at a few miles' distance were heard; and at night, flashes of lightning seemed sometimes to break from the earth. For two or three months the shocks were frequent; almost every day. Then they gradually decreased in frequency and took place at longer intervals, which continued to lengthen till they finally ceased. In May 1817, in Tennessee, they had come to be several months apart and were but just perceptible. The last of them was in 1822.

Judge Haywood lived in Nashville at the time of the earthquakes. An even more graphic description of them is given by a resident of New Madrid, Mrs. Eliza Bryan, who wrote in 1816 that:

On the 16th of December, 1811, about 2 o'clock a.m.,
a violent shock of earthquake, accompanied by a very
loud noise, resembling loud but distant thunder, but
hoarse and vibrating, followed by complete saturation
of the atmosphere with sulphurous vapor causing total
darkness. The screams of the inhabitants, the cries of the
fowles and beasts of every species, the falling trees, and
the roaring of the Mississippi, the current of which was
retrograde for a few minutes, owing, as it is supposed, to
an eruption in its bed, formed a scene truly horrible.

Mrs. Bryan further revealed that minor rumblings continued until January 23, 1812, when another quake, every bit as violent as the one of December 16, occurred. "The Mississippi first seemed to recede from its banks," she declared, adding that the turmoil left "many boats, which were on their way to New Orleans, on the bare sand, in which time the poor sailors made their escape from them."

Finally, on February 7, 1812, the most severe quake of all hit the middle Mississippi River valley. Vibrations from this one were felt over practically the entire eastern United States, an area encompassing one and a half million square miles. Yet, as violent and devastating as all of the New Madrid earthquakes were, very few humans lost their lives, primarily because the region was so sparsely populated.

One of the most impressive, still-visible remnants of the New Madrid earthquakes of 1811–1812 is Reelfoot Lake, located in the northwest corner of Tennessee, just across the Mississippi from the town of New Madrid, Missouri, the supposed epicenter of the quakes. Erroneously described by Mrs. Bryan in 1816 as "upwards of 100 miles long and from one to six miles wide, of a depth of from 10 to 50 feet," the lake today has had a great deal of its water surface reclaimed by land. Present-day Reelfoot covers about twenty thousand acres and measures about fourteen by five miles.

The sight of Reelfoot Lake, with its ancient cypress trees—many of them topped with American eagle nests—is a stark reminder of just how violent Nature can be. And, it also generates thoughts of how this part of the Mississippi River valley would fare today if another New Madrid earthquake were to hit. Millions of people inhabit the land encompassed along a five hundred mile radius from the epicenter. There is little question, that if tremors of an equivalent magnitude as the 1811–1812 quakes ever come again, the loss of human and animal life and the destruction of property will be almost unfathomable.

THE FIRST STEAMBOAT ON THE MISSISSIPPI RIVER

- 1812 -

January 10, 1812, was a special day for the several hundred residents of New Orleans. For days, they had received reports from upriver that a mighty new type of river craft was on its way downstream to dock at their town. It was called a steamboat, and it was powered by the steam manufactured from boiling water. As scores of anxious spectators, led by Governor Charles C. C. Claiborne himself, gathered at the wharf, many wondered how such a machine could possibly work. No doubt, not a few snickered among themselves that the new type of boat would never be popular and certainly would never replace the hundreds of flatboats that frequented the river every year.

The notion that boats could be powered by steam was the idea of a New York entrepreneur named Robert Fulton. He had demonstrated almost five years earlier that such a watercraft was feasible when his newly designed steamboat, the *Clermont*, made the trip between New York City and Albany—a distance of one hundred and fifty miles—in thirty-two hours. But, there were many detractors. Fulton sadly wrote later that,

> *The morning I left New York, there were not perhaps*
> *thirty persons in the city who believed that the boat*
> *would ever move one mile an hour, or be of the least*
> *utility, and while we were putting off from the wharf,*
> *which was crowded with spectators, I heard a number*
> *of sarcastic remarks.*

Fulton was jubilant over the success of the *Clermont*. His real interests, however, were in implementing steamboats on the western waters, particularly the Mississippi, where he knew thousands of pounds of produce and other products were annually shipped downstream. What a difference could be made by utilizing a craft that would navigate back upstream almost as fast as it floated downstream. What a savings to the people who laboriously built flatboats and other primitive craft to float their wares downstream, and who, once they had arrived at their destination, were required to break up the boats for lumber and walk back home. Steamboats, declared Fulton, will "give a cheap and quick conveyance to the merchandise on the Mississippi, Missouri and other great rivers, which are now laying open their treasures to the enterprise of our countrymen."

Before committing to the Mississippi River steamboat business, Fulton and his financial backer, Robert Livingston, hired a young man, Nicholas Roosevelt, an early kinsman of the presidential Roosevelts, to study the western waterways and to report back to them with his findings and recommendations about whether such a commercial endeavor could or should be achieved. Roosevelt, along with his bride of six months, left Pittsburgh during the summer of 1809 aboard a luxurious flatboat that Roosevelt himself had built.

The boat was described by Mrs. Roosevelt as having "a comfortable bed room, dining room, pantry, and a room in front for the crew, with a fire-place where the cooking was done."

The Roosevelt party arrived in New Orleans in December and Nicholas and his wife returned to New York the following month. Roosevelt immediately gave a favorable report to Fulton and Livingston, who lost no time in forming the Ohio Steamboat Navigation Company, under whose auspices they would run their vast western shipping empire. Roosevelt, in the meantime, traveled to Pittsburgh, built a boat yard, and commenced work on the maiden steamboat that would visit New Orleans and points downstream.

When Roosevelt's steamboat was launched from his Pittsburgh boat yard in March 1811, it was christened the *New Orleans,* in honor of the city at the end of its proposed voyage. The boat, built at a cost of $38,000, measured nearly one hundred and fifty feet by thirty-three feet, had a hold of twelve feet, and was capable of hauling between three and four hundred tons. In addition to the side-wheel powered by the steam engine, it was equipped with two masts that could be used with sails in case of mechanical failure.

The big day came on October 20, 1811, and as hundreds of wide-eyed spectators looked on, the *New Orleans* quietly slipped its mooring ropes and glided into the Monongahela River. In addition to Roosevelt and his faithful wife, Lydia, the crew consisted of an engineer, a pilot, "six hands, two female servants, a man waiter, a cook, and an immense Newfoundland dog, named Tiger."

Only sixty-four hours were required to make the trip from Pittsburgh to Louisville, and the *New Orleans* averaged eight to ten miles per hour. When the Falls of the Ohio were reached at Louisville, the water was too shallow for passage, so Roosevelt conducted tours back and forth to Cincinnati to the delight of scores of enthralled observers. When heavy rains came, thus allowing the boat to pass the Falls, Mrs.

Roosevelt bore her second child, and a determined Lydia, with babe in arms, watched from the pilot's house as the *New Orleans* gracefully began its forty-five minute trip over the cataract.

In mid-December 1811, as the *New Orleans* and her crew approached the confluence of the Ohio and Mississippi Rivers, all on board felt the effects of what proved to be initial shocks from the New Madrid earthquake. As they continued downriver and finally turned south into the Mississippi, evidence of the earthquake's fury was visible everywhere. And, there was much more excitement. Shortly after entering the Mississippi, several canoe loads of hostile Chickasaw Indians pursued the *New Orleans* for what seemed to Lydia like an eternity, before the steamboat's superior speed outpaced them. Then, a few more miles downstream, Roosevelt awakened during the night to find one of the boat's cabins on fire.

A little time later, at the village of New Madrid, Missouri, which later was discovered to be the epicenter for the tremors, scores of terrified townspeople begged Roosevelt to let them onboard. Sadly, however, for his own family's and crew's safety, he had to refuse. Mrs. Roosevelt lamented that she "lived in a constant fright, unable to sleep or sew, or read."

Finally, the *New Orleans* escaped harm's way and pulled up to the wharf at Natchez. On January 10, 1812, eighty-two days out of Pittsburgh, the packet and its proud passengers and crew arrived at New Orleans. Out of those nearly two thousand hours on the river, less than two hundred and sixty of them were actual running time. Roosevelt was elated. He and his partners had proven once and for all that steamboats provided a fast, reliable, and comfortable means of transportation and communication along America's inland waterway system. As for the fate of the *New Orleans,* it snagged two years later on a submerged tree trunk just above Baton Rouge and sank in the muddy waters of the Mississippi River.

THE BATTLE OF NEW ORLEANS

- 1815 -

Whenever the War of 1812 is discussed, the clash that usually comes to most people's minds is the Battle of New Orleans. The conflict occurred on January 8, 1815, ironically, two weeks *after* representatives of the United States and Great Britain had signed the peace treaty ending the war. However, neither General Andrew Jackson nor British general Sir Edward Pakenham, the opposing commanders, was aware of the fact.

America's second conflict with Great Britain had officially begun on June 18, 1812, when a reluctant Congress voted seventy-nine to forty-nine in the House and nineteen to thirteen in the Senate to declare war. Affairs between the two nations had been deteriorating for several years, precipitated primarily by the British policy of impressment, or seizure, of American seamen on the high seas.

The British navy about this time was experiencing a heavy loss of its own sailors through desertion. In order to reduce its attrition rate, the Royal Navy implemented a policy of searching American vessels on the high seas for its runaway sailors. The U.S. government protested the action, especially since, in many cases, the British not only reclaimed their own subjects, but seized numerous American citizens as well.

When a group of young, newly elected congressmen known as the War Hawks—John C. Calhoun of South Carolina, Felix Grundy of Tennessee, and Henry Clay of Kentucky—vocalized their grave concerns over this violation of maritime law, they quickly captured the nation's attention from the more conservative peace factions and set the stage for the ensuing conflict.

In July, following the declaration of war, General William Hull, the governor of Michigan Territory, invaded Canada. Fearing that his communications with Detroit would be cut by the British, he quickly retreated across the border after learning that Fort Michili-mackinac had surrendered peaceably. On August 16, Detroit surrendered to British troops, and Michigan and the upper Mississippi River valley fell temporarily under British control.

During the course of the conflict, considerable action took place around the Great Lakes and along the eastern seaboard. Finally, on August 25, 1813, the British invaded Washington and burned both the Capitol and the President's House. Eighteen days later, redcoats assaulted Baltimore, but the success of Fort McHenry in protecting the city doomed the attempt to failure.

The city of New Orleans was the prize in the South. British military planners decided it was absolutely necessary to capture the port at the mouth of the Mississippi River so they could exercise complete control over the stream, thereby restricting use of the river or the port facilities at New Orleans to inland American farmers who had no other outlet for their products.

At New Orleans, during a two-week period in late 1814 and early 1815, besieged Americans, under the command of Andrew Jackson, confronted a superior British army led by Sir Edward Pakenham. Jackson deployed his army of Tennesseans, Kentuckians, pirates, blacks, Indians, and Creoles along the dried-up Rodriguez Canal. Heavy British artillery fire failed to dislodge them, so Pakenham ordered his 5,400 veteran soldiers of the Crown to attack Jackson's defenses head-on. The British troops became easy targets for Jackson's ragtag army, and the Battle of New Orleans was won in thirty minutes. More than two thousand British soldiers were killed during the brief encounter, while Jackson lost only thirteen Americans.

The two commanders at New Orleans were as different as daylight and dark. Jackson, a product of the wild frontier, had just recently distinguished himself by overcoming the Creek Indians in Alabama. He had moved to Nashville, Tennessee, in the late 1780s and had filled several public offices including attorney general for the Western District of North Carolina (present-day Tennessee), U.S. congressman, U.S. senator, and major-general of the Tennessee militia. Now, the forty-seven-year-old veteran was a major-general in the regular army.

Pakenham, on the other hand, had been brought up in a well-to-do family and had been trained in the classic European school of warfare. He was rudely awakened by the unorthodox methods of fighting displayed by Jackson's Tennesseans and other troops. Organized, well-disciplined, "follow-the-leader" soldiers had no place in the swamps of Louisiana, a point well-taken by Pakenham as he observed hundreds of his red-coated troopers fall to the ground in heaps before the blistering fire of the Americans. A few minutes into the fight, Pakenham himself was killed. Years later, Jackson recalled the event and related the circumstances of his adversary's death.

*I heard a single rifle shot from a group of country carts
we had been using, and a moment thereafter I saw*

Pakenham reel and pitch out of his saddle . . . . I did
not know where General Pakenham was lying or I
should have sent to him, or gone to him in person, to
offer any service in my power to render. I was told he
lived two hours after he was hit.

The affair at New Orleans catapulted Andrew Jackson into the
public limelight. Theodore Roosevelt, in his maritime study, *Naval
War of 1812,* wrote that:

The American soldiers deserve great credit for doing so
well; but greater credit still belongs to Andrew Jackson,
who, with his cool hand, stands out in history as the
ablest general the United States produced from the out-
break of the Revolution down to the beginning of the
Great Rebellion.

The War of 1812 lasted for thirty months. Despite the large loss
of life and property on both sides, the war accomplished little, and
when it was finally over the strained relationships between the two
combatants were no different than they were before the war.

FORT SNELLING AND THE
BEGINNINGS OF
MINNEAPOLIS-ST. PAUL

1820

In 1679 Father Louis Hennepin, a Jesuit priest who was part of the entourage of the French explorer, La Salle, stood on the banks of the Mississippi River in present-day Minnesota and observed for the first time a series of magnificent cataracts which he named the Falls of St. Anthony. For the next eighty years, French influence—in the guise of fur trappers, traders, and voyageurs—spread throughout the western Great Lakes region, only to be abruptly ended when France was expelled from most of North America at the termination of the French and Indian War. Its place was taken by the British, who carried on an aggressive fur trade with the Indian inhabitants of the vast region through the auspices of the North West Company.

As early as 1805, United States authorities expressed concern over the influence that British traders had among the various Indian tribes living along the headwaters of the Mississippi River. That year, General James Wilkinson, the commander of the U.S. army stationed at St. Louis, sent Lieutenant Zebulon Pike up the river to visit with and to establish relations among the Sioux Indians who maintained homes around the Falls of St. Anthony. If several plots of land could be secured from the Indians, the plan was for the army to build a series of military posts scattered throughout the region.

Pike's mission was successful, and he purchased a tract of property described as:

> . . . *nine miles square at the mouth of the St. Croix,*
> *also, from below the confluence of the Mississippi and*
> *St. Peter's, up the Mississippi, to include the Falls of St.*
> *Anthony, extending nine miles on each side of the river.*

The tract consisted of nearly 156,000 acres, most of it located in the vicinity of the Falls. The Sioux received $2,000 as full payment for the property. As events turned out, all of Pike's efforts were for naught. Other military matters were more pressing, and nothing was done with the property for another fourteen years.

In the meantime, the United States and Great Britain fought the War of 1812, and although the United States emerged the winner, the victory did little to diminish British influence among the northwestern Indian tribes. Accordingly, in 1819, in an attempt to neutralize British authority once and for all, the army sent Colonel Henry Leavenworth, commander of the Fifth Infantry, to establish a post, named Cantonment New Hope, on the south bank of the Minnesota River at its confluence with the Mississippi.

The site selection for the new fort was a bad one, and during the first winter, several soldiers died from a scurvy epidemic. During the following spring, Leavenworth abandoned the post and began construction on a new one, which he christened Fort St. Anthony, on the opposite bank of the Minnesota. There, he hoped his garrison could fulfill its orders, issued by secretary of war John C. Calhoun to encourage "the enlargement and protection of our fur trade," and to maintain "the permanent peace of our North Western frontier, by Securing a decided control over the various tribes of Indians in that quarter." Before Colonel Leavenworth became too deeply involved in the building of the new post, he was replaced by Colonel Josiah Snelling. Five years later, the fort was renamed Fort Snelling in his honor.

Fort Snelling was a magnificent structure. Built of native stone, with massive blockhouses located at each corner, the bastion was equipped with artillery along its walls. Inside the compound were housed the barracks, powder magazine, stables, and mess hall for the soldiers, as well as the first school, circulating library, and hospital in the western Great Lakes country. But, the fortification had its critics. Colonel George Croghan, the U.S. Army's inspector-general, visited the post, as well as others in the vicinity, on a regular basis. During his 1827 stopover, he wrote that:

I know not by whom the lines of this fort were first traced, nor can I state at what expenditure of public funds the work has been thus far advanced, but of these facts I am confident that it might have been contracted for at a much less cost, that it covers an extent of ground too large by three fourths for any garrison that can be permanently given it, and that it has deprived Colonel Snelling of the satisfaction of having a command that might fairly compare in degree of instruction with any other in service.

On the other hand, Croghan was highly complimentary of the living conditions at the fort. Eleven years later, on a subsequent inspection tour, he commented that:

> *No soldiers ought to desire to live better than they have always done at this post. The government ration is sufficient of itself, and to it may be added the abundant supply of vegetables at all times to be had from the gardens of the several companies.*

Fort Snelling was continuously occupied by the Army until 1858, when the troops were withdrawn, only to return during the War Between the States. After the War, the post maintained its military presence in the region until 1946, when the property was turned over to the Veterans Administration. In the meantime, a fur-trading post at nearby Mendota had grown in size until, by 1841, its population merited the establishment of a Jesuit mission that was named after the Apostle Paul. By 1849, with a population of 642, St. Paul was selected as the territorial capital of Minnesota. Rapid growth sent the town's population soaring to ten thousand by 1854, when it was officially incorporated. Four years later the city became the capital of the state of Minnesota.

During the same general period, in 1838, a village named St. Anthony was settled near the Falls on the east side of the Mississippi and, eleven years later, Minneapolis was established across the river. When the two towns merged in 1872, the present-day city of Minneapolis-St. Paul was born.

Because of their strategic location on the Mississippi River, the twin cities of Minneapolis-St. Paul transformed rapidly into important commercial and transportation centers. The power generated from the Falls of St. Anthony helped make Minneapolis the home to many large lumber and grain mills. St. Paul, with a great deal of thanks to James J. Hill, the railroad magnate, grew rapidly as a rail hub for the northern roads linking the Great Lakes with the Pacific Ocean.

FRANCES WRIGHT'S VISION

- 1826 -

The early 1800s found many utopian colonies operating across the United States. An early one was Robert Owen's New Harmony experiment, founded in 1825 in the farmlands of extreme southwestern Indiana. A lesser-known community was Nashoba, organized just a few miles from Memphis, Tennessee, and the banks of the Mississippi River.

Nashoba's founding genius was a British woman named Frances (Fanny) Wright. Born in 1795 in Dundee, Scotland, Fanny was orphaned at a young age and raised by English relatives. Well educated for a female of the period, Wright soon fell under the influence of French materialism philosophies, and during her early twenties, she became an outspoken disciple of utopianism, women's rights, free love, and other radical—for the times, at least—movements.

When Fanny was twenty-three years old, she and her sister, Camilla, traveled to the United States. What the two self-declared reformers found in the towns and countryside of rural America was a ready-made platform for their philosophies and beliefs. Fanny unsuccessfully tried her hand at writing and producing a play in New York City in 1819, the plot of which gravitated around Swiss independence. Two years later, she published a popular book entitled *Views of Society and Manners in America,* a study that captured the attention of European radical reformers, including the French hero of the American Revolution, the Marquis de Lafayette.

Lafayette's influence on the Wright sisters led them to formulate and launch a new enterprise in the United States. During her earlier American travels, Fanny had never toured the South, primarily because of her abhorrence of slavery. Now, she decided that she not only would visit the region, but she aspired to become a spokesman for abolition and to establish a colony for freed slaves as well. Edd Winfield Parks, a prominent Tennessee historian and biographer, best described the project when he wrote in 1932 that Fanny's proposed utopia would

> . . . *educate and . . . emancipate the slaves. But the work must be done gradually. Her . . . colony would be based on a system of cooperative labor, the slaves bought in whole families. Within five years, she figured, the labor of the slaves would pay for their original cost, including six per cent interest on the capital, and for their keep. In this period the older slaves could be taught a trade, taught at least to read, to figure, and to write: the children could be given a complete rudimentary education. Absolute and immediate abolition might be productive of great evil: this gradual emancipation, with careful teaching . . . would benefit not only the*

*slaves, but the white people. White immigrants would
take the place of the negroes, who might be colonized in
Haiti, Texas, or California, where they could work out
a civilization of their own.*

Apparently it never occurred to Miss Wright that within a few
years Texas and California would be integral parts of the United
States, vital factors in the menacing issue of slavery.

In September 1825, with grandiose ideas in her mind, and with
$17,000 in her pocketbook, Fanny Wright arrived in Nashville and
met with General Andrew Jackson, who was, at the time, active in
land speculation in the far western part of Tennessee. Jackson—
along with his one-time law partner, John Overton, and General
James Winchester—had founded Memphis in Shelby County on
the banks of the Mississippi River only six years earlier. Now, Old
Hickory was anxious to dispose of as much Shelby County land as
he could. He directed Fanny to his friends, William Lawrence and
William A. Davis, from whom the colonizer purchased three hundred acres of marshy woodland along the Wolf River. According to
historian Parks, Wright christened her new home, "Nashoba, the old
Chickasaw name for wolf."

Within six months of the land purchase, the Nashoba colony
had started off with a bang. Two large log houses were built.
Fanny, Camilla, and the sisters' white followers occupied one,
while the several slaves they had bought in Nashville set up house-
keeping in the other. During the next year, more land was acquired
and cleared, several other cabins were built, and Fanny came
down with a severe case of malaria. In an attempt to recuperate
as rapidly as possible, she was forced to move north to the cooler
climate of New Albany, Indiana. In her absence, Nashoba fell on
hard times.

Sister Camilla, who had taken over the job of teaching both young and old slaves, found her subjects difficult to deal with. Little work was done by anybody, and the project just rocked along, making little progress for the next several months. One year after its founding, a disappointed visitor described Nashoba's surroundings as "second-rate land, and scarcely a hundred acres of it cleared: three or four squared log houses, and a few cabins for the slaves, the only buildings; slaves released from the fear of the lash, working indolently . . . . "

Fanny now returned to Europe, hoping to drum up support and additional dollars for her noble Tennessee experiment. In her absence, the direction of the operations took a different turn, leaving the poor, ignorant slaves as the real victims of the misdirected project. The original bylaws of Nashoba stipulated that before a slave could be emancipated, the fruits of his labor must pay the organization a total of $6,000 plus his living expenses. Now, to make matters worse, severe restrictions were placed upon those in bondage, making many wonder whether slavery itself was not a better fate. Two of the rules were particularly offensive to the slaves. One dictated that they "not be allowed to receive money, clothing, food, or indeed anything whatever from any person resident at, or visiting this place," while another one demanded that "the slaves . . . not be permitted to eat elsewhere than at the public meals . . . . "

Wright revisited Nashoba in 1828, full of fresh vigor and new expectations for her slave colony. But, gradually, the malarial climate, the lack of money, and a decided cooling of the fervor originally demonstrated by the Wright sisters, closed the doors on the gone-astray utopian colony. Fanny spent a final season in Tennessee, freed all the remaining slaves, and moved to New Harmony, Indiana. In her biography, published in 1844, she admitted failure, writing that "for the first time she bowed her head in humility before the omnipotence of collective humanity."

Fanny lived for another twenty-two years after her failure at Nashoba. During that period of her life, she traveled the American lecture tour, wrote widely of her radical philosophies, married, gave birth to a daughter, and separated from her husband. She lived in retirement in Cincinnati, Ohio, until her death in 1852. Perhaps the *American Cyclopedia of Biography* best described this courageous, if not somewhat misled, woman when its biographer wrote, "She was benevolent, unselfish, eccentric, and fearless."

BLACK HAWK'S WAR

- 1832 -

Black Hawk was a thirty-seven-year-old Sac (sometimes called Sauk) warrior in late 1804, when a number of the chiefs and elders of his tribe journeyed to St. Louis to treaty with the United States government. Representing the U.S. War Department was the governor of Indiana Territory, William Henry Harrison. When the proceedings were completed, the Sac tribe and its neighbor, the Fox, had relinquished nearly fifty million acres of land stretching on both sides of the Mississippi River between the mouths of the Wisconsin and Illinois Rivers for $1,000 a year in trade goods.

Article VII of the 1804 treaty stated that "as long as the lands which are now ceded to the United States remain their property, the Indians belonging to the said tribes shall enjoy the privilege of living and hunting upon them." The provision made sense at the time when only a few thousand settlers lived in the entire upper Mississippi River valley. But, by the 1830s, when hundreds of American families were pouring into the region to establish farms in the rich woodlands and prairies, Article VII became just another idle guarantee made to the Indians that had no meaning for the land-hungry farmers.

In the meantime, Black Hawk had become more and more leery of the Americans. He never considered the earlier treaty to be legal and, a few years after the great land giveaway of 1804, he joined the Shawnee leader, Tecumseh, and fought with his Indian confederation against the United States in the War of 1812. He shared with the readers of his autobiography, *The Life of Black Hawk,* published in 1834, his distrust of all things American, when he wrote,

> *I had not discovered one good trait in the character*
> *of the Americans that had come to the country! They*
> *made fair promises, but never fulfilled them! Whilst the*
> *British made but few—but we could always rely upon*
> *their word!*

By the late 1820s, several American families had settled upon the Sac lands bordering the east side of the Mississippi River. In fact, one farmer had actually established a household in Black Hawk's own abode! Black Hawk told the man "not to settle on our lands—not trouble our lodges or fences—that there was plenty of land in the country for them to settle upon—and they must leave our village, as we were coming back to it in the spring." Black Hawk, now a tribal chief, waited for three long years for American authorities to discipline the unwanted settlers and to force them to withdraw from their village. For three years, no action was taken.

In early 1832, Black Hawk finally decided to take matters into his own hands. He crossed the Mississippi River (he and his small band had wintered on the west side of the stream) with about one thousand followers, intent on re-occupying their village. General Edmund P. Gaines, commander of the Western Department of the U.S. Army and an old veteran of the Creek and Seminole campaigns, was ordered to meet Black Hawk head on.

With Gaines's contingent of regular army troops were about sixteen hundred Illinois volunteers, who had been hastily called up by Governor John Reynolds. On May 14, 1832, when several hundred of these Illinois militia, led by Major Isaiah Stillman, attacked Black Hawk and forty braves who were separated from the Sac camp and the rest of the warriors, Black Hawk decided to surrender to the superior force. However, instead of honoring the chief's white flag, Stillman's volunteers began shooting into the ranks. At this point, Black Hawk ordered an attack of his own, and his warriors reacted so viciously that Stillman's militia was forced to retreat. Black Hawk wrote disgustedly of the affair in his autobiography.

Never was I so much surprised in my life, as I was in this attack! An army of three or four hundred, after having learned that we were sueing [sic] for peace, to attempt to kill the flag-bears that had gone, unarmed, to ask for a meeting of the war chiefs of the two contending parties to hold a council . . . to come forward, with a full determination to demolish the few braves I had with me, to retreat when they had ten to one, was unaccountable to me. It proved a different spirit from any I had ever before seen among the pale faces! I expected to see them fight as the Americans did with the British during the last war!—but they had no braves among them!

The embarrassing affair, which occurred in Ogle County, Illinois, was forever afterward called the Battle of Stillman's Run.

The sight of Stillman's men hastily retreating gave Black Hawk renewed optimism, and he proceeded to lay waste to the surrounding region. His victories were short-lived, however. By summer, the Army, supported by militias from several nearby states, had the Sacs and their Fox allies pinned to the east bank of the Mississippi River. Black Hawk had no choice but to retreat across the river to Iowa.

In early August, he gathered his following near the confluence of the Bad Axe and Mississippi Rivers. There, he intended to surrender and to publicly announce that he was leading his people to the far side of the Mississippi. Before he could do so, however, the steamship, *Warrior,* arrived and a brief engagement ensued. The next day, as the majority of his people tried to cross the river, a large contingent of American army troops appeared on the scene. Despite the white flag flying over the Indians' temporary camp, the soldiers commenced firing. Two years later, Black Hawk described the slaughter in his book.

> *Early in the morning a party of whites . . . came upon our people, who were attempting to cross the Mississippi. They tried to give themselves up—the whites paid no attention to their entreaties—but commenced slaughtering them! In a little while the whole army arrived. Our braves, but few in number, finding that the enemy paid no regard to age or sex, and seeing that they were murdering helpless women and little children, determined to fight until they were killed! As many women as could, commenced swimming the Mississippi, with their children on their backs. A number*

*of them were drowned, and some shot, before they could
reach the opposite shore.*

*To make matters worse, a great number of those
lucky enough to safely swim the river were slaughtered
as they came out of the water on the far side by Sioux
Indian allies of the army.*

The massacre at the mouth of the Bad Axe River ended the
brief, but bloody, Black Hawk War. Black Hawk himself was taken
prisoner and paraded all over the East as an example of the defeated
red man. He was later released, accepted the inevitability that he now
lived in a white man's world, wrote his autobiography, and finally
died in Iowa in 1838.

DISCOVERING THE SOURCE OF THE
MISSISSIPPI RIVER

- 1832 -

The Mississippi River was one of the first major natural features that European explorers "discovered" during their early ramblings across North America. Yet, from the time that Hernando De Soto initially saw the river near the site of present-day Memphis, Tennessee, in 1541, the actual source of the mighty stream remained elusive for nearly three hundred years.

From their earliest arrival in the Great Lakes region, French missionaries, fur trappers, and traders had often frequented parts of the upper Mississippi River. However, the section of the stream stretching northward from the Falls of St. Anthony—nearly six hundred miles—was left undisturbed and consigned to the Chippewas and other Indians who claimed the area as home.

By around the turn of the nineteeth century, the vast Minnesota region was in the path of American exploitation and settlement. Before long, a natural curiosity developed over the exact source of the Mississippi River. In 1798, a Canadian explorer attacked the task first. David Thompson, a trader employed with the North West Company, a Canadian-based fur establishment, claimed he had located the true source of the river in Turtle Lake, located in northern Minnesota.

In 1806, the Americans got in on the search. During December of that year, in the middle of a harsh Minnesota winter, Lieutenant Zebulon M. Pike of the United States army got fairly close to the river's source when he arrived at Leech Lake, situated several score miles from the point known today to be the real beginning of the Mississippi. Less than twenty years later, on two separate journeys, Michigan governor Lewis Cass and an Italian romantic named Giacomo C. Beltrami both flirted with success as well, but in the end they failed to discover the river's source just as Thompson and Pike had.

Accompanying Governor Cass on his 1820 expedition was a twenty-seven-year-old mineralogist named Henry Rowe Schoolcraft. Twelve years later, in 1832, when he got the chance to launch his own search for the source of the Mississippi, Schoolcraft grasped the opportunity with relish. By then, he was employed as an Indian agent for the United States War Department, with responsibilities that included the welfare of the Chippewa and Sioux tribes of upper Minnesota.

With orders to "proceed to the country upon the heads of the Mississippi, and visit as many of the Indians in that, and the intermediate region, as circumstances will permit," Schoolcraft set out on a journey that would forever link his name with the Mississippi River. He was accompanied by an eleven-man army detachment, a surgeon, a missionary, an interpreter, and several French laborers, or *engages*. By early July, the group had reached Cass Lake, which Schoolcraft believed to be in the general vicinity of the river's source.

There, "distributed among five canoes, with provisions for ten days, a tent and poles, oil cloth, mess basket, tea-kettle, flag and a staff, a medicine chest, some instruments, an herbarium, fowling pieces, and a few Indian presents," Schoolcraft, a Chippewa Indian guide named "The Yellowhead," and fourteen other companions began the search in earnest.

After marching through what seemed like miles of marshy lowland and completing a back-breaking, six-mile portage, the small exploring party finally reached their long-sought-after destination— Elk Lake, called by the French, *Lac la Biche*. In his book describing the incident, Schoolcraft later wrote that the lake

> *is, in every respect, a beautiful sheet of water, seven*
> *or eight miles in extent, lying among hills of diluvial*
> *formation, surmounted with pines, which fringe the*
> *distant horizon . . . . The waters are transparent and*
> *bright, and reflect a foliage produced by the elm, lynn,*
> *maple, and cherry . . . .*

Measuring a tiny stream that poured forth from the lake, Schoolcraft found the rivulet to be " . . . perhaps ten to twelve feet broad, with an apparent depth of twelve to eighteen inches." This, he proudly declared, was the birthplace of the Mississippi River. Scouring the landscape, the group discovered a single island in the middle of the lake and christened it Schoolcraft Island. Upon its rocky shores, they planted the flagstaff and proudly raised the American flag high above the small trees that populated the landscape.

Convinced that he had located the true source of the Mississippi River, Schoolcraft and his small following departed Elk Lake after only three hours of exploration in the vicinity. He was still on government business, and his official negotiations with the Chippewas and the Sioux had priority over his personal desire to stay longer at this historic place. But, he decided, there was one thing he must do: he had to rename Elk Lake. Future maps must reflect a properly respectful name for the body of water that gave birth to the largest river in America.

As he left the vicinity, Schoolcraft asked his missionary companion, William T. Boutwell, if he could think of a Latin or Greek name that might be bestowed upon the lake to signify that it was, indeed, the source of the mighty Mississippi. Boutwell suggested the Latin words, *veritas* and *caput,* meaning "truth" and "head." After some thought, Schoolcraft decided to take the "itas" out of "veritas" and to combine it with the "ca" out of "caput" to come up with "Itasca." That was it! From that time forward, his discovery would be known as Lake Itasca. And so, in this manner, did the source of the "Father of Waters" receive its name.

GEORGE CATLIN
AND THE PIPESTONE QUARRY

- 1836 -

The decade of the 1830s witnessed three outstanding artists—George Catlin, Karl Bodmer, and Alfred Jacob Miller—wandering the vast wilderness of the trans-Mississippi, intent on graphically capturing the lifestyles of the Plains-dwelling Indians before they were corrupted by rapidly approaching civilization. Each man returned to the East with hundreds of sketches and paintings.

George Catlin was the first of the three to make the trip West. Born in 1796 in Wilkes-Barre, Pennsylvania, Catlin was engrossed as a child by tales told to him by his mother, a one-time captive of the Indians. Trained as an attorney, he was ill suited to the lifestyle of a barrister, so when he was around twenty-seven years old, he gave up his law practice, moved to Philadelphia, and began painting portraits for a living. Within a year of his career move, he was recognized among his new peers and elected to the prestigious Pennsylvania Academy of Fine Arts.

Although he enjoyed painting, he became disenchanted with his job of portraitist and yearned for something more exciting. "My mind was continually reaching for some branch or enterprise of the arts, on which to devote a whole life-time of enthusiasm," he lamented. After observing a delegation of American Indians visiting in Philadelphia, Catlin resolved that "the history and customs of such a people preserved by pictorial illustration are themes worthy the life-time of one man, and nothing short of the loss of my life shall prevent me from visiting their country and becoming their historian."

Catlin took his first trip to the West in 1832, all the way to Fort Union aboard the steamboat *Yellowstone.* Subsequent journeys in 1834 to visit the tribes of the southern Great Plains and in 1835 to paint the natives of the upper Mississippi River region provided the artist with hundreds of subjects to paint, and he worked feverishly to get all of his work accomplished. It was his last trip, however, the one in 1836, that carried him to Minnesota's famed Pipestone Quarry, ended Catlin's career as a painter, and launched his second calling as promoter of his own art.

During all of his three previous forays west, he had been intrigued by the great amount of the beautiful, reddish-colored pipestone that members of the various tribes used in the manufacture of their calumets and pipes. Whenever one of the smokers was questioned, the answer regarding the stone's origin was always the same—it came from a sacred quarry located in the southwestern corner of present-day Minnesota. Before returning to the East and the job of marketing his canvasses, Catlin resolved to visit the mysterious rock quarry.

Catlin and a companion neared the quarry in late summer, 1836. After being threatened by Sioux Indians not to go near the place, the hard-headed Catlin proceeded anyway and, as it turned out, safely. In so doing, he became the first white man of record to view the awesome sight. Later, he wrote of his first encounter with the magnificent wonderland.

On the very top of this mound or ridge, we found the far-famed quarry or fountain of the Red Pipe, which is truly an anomaly in nature. The principal and most striking feature of this place, is a perpendicular wall of close-grained, compact quartz, of twenty-five and thirty feet in elevation, running nearly North and South with its face to the West, exhibiting a front of nearly two miles in length, when it disappears at both ends by running under the prairie . . . . The depression of the brow of the ridge at this place has been caused by the wash of a little stream, produced by several springs on the top, a little back from the Wall; which has gradually carried away the super-incumbent earth, and having bared the wall for the distance of two miles, is now left to glide for some distance over a perfectly level surface of quartz rock . . . .

This beautiful wall is horizontal, and stratified in several distinct layers of light grey [sic], and rose or flesh-coloured quartz; and for most of the way, both on the front of the wall, and for acres of its horizontal surface, highly polished or glazed, as if by ignition.

At the base of this wall there is a level prairie, of half a mile in width, running parallel to it; in any and all parts of which, the Indians procure the red stone for their pipes, by digging through the soil and several slaty layers of the red stone, to the depth of four or five feet. From the very numerous marks of ancient and modern diggings or excavations, it would appear that this place has been for many centuries resorted to for the red stone; and from

the great number of graves and remains of ancient for-
tifications in its vicinity, it would seem, as well as from
their actual traditions, that the Indian tribes have long
held this place in high superstitious estimation; and also
that it has been the resort of different tribes, who have
made their regular pilgrimages here to renew their pipes
. . . .

While at the quarry, Catlin collected samples of pipestone and passed them on to the scientific community back East, which declared it "a new mineral compound." It was labeled catlinite in honor of the painter.

When Catlin retired from active painting, he toured extensively across the eastern United States and on the Continent. His traveling "Indian Gallery," as he called the huge collection of paintings and drawings of his beloved natives, showed to enthusiastic crowds in New York, Washington, D.C., Baltimore, Philadelphia, and Boston, before being taken to Europe in 1840. There, for the next several years, his work was displayed in London, Paris, and Brussels. In the meantime, unable to raise money by persuading the federal government to purchase his Indian Gallery, he had fallen on hard times. His wife died, and he traveled extensively throughout South America before finally returning to the United States in 1870.

Catlin died in 1872 at the age of seventy-seven. At the time, the fate of his beloved Indian Gallery was still uncertain. The U.S. government steadfastly refused to purchase it, but nearly seven years later, the remaining collection was finally acquired by the Smithsonian Institution, through the courtesy of a private donor. Today, several of the artist's most famous paintings hang in Washington's National Gallery of Art, where they are viewed by hundreds of thousands of admirers annually.

DAVY CROCKETT'S
MISSISSIPPI RIVER EXPLOITS

- 1837 -

There can be little doubt that David Crockett was one of America's all-time popular folk heroes. Born in present-day East Tennessee in 1786, Davy received very little formal education. During his Tennessee years, he moved all over the state, served in the Creek War of 1813–1814, sat in the Tennessee Legislature, and was sent to Washington as a United States congressman. When he was defeated in a final try for the House of Representatives, he moved to Texas where he was killed at the Alamo in March 1836.

Crockett was a legend in his own time. Even before his death at the Alamo permanently fixed him in the public mind, stories were being told about his many feats of derring-do. Following his demise in Texas, one of the vehicles that helped make Crockett immortal was *Davy Crockett's Almanac,* published for a number of years in Nashville. The fictional stories in the *Almanacs* were written in the first person by other people, but all of them are obviously tall tales, as will be seen from the following story, published in 1837, describing how Crockett swam the Mississippi River. Here is the story in his own words, narrated by the legend himself. Of course, much of the interest, humor, and color of the story lie in the rude grammar used by the narrator, so nothing has been changed from the original.

Of all the rivers on this airth, the Mississippi beats all holler. Many a tough time have I had in swimming across its turbid waters. I always rubbed myself thoroughly with skunk's grease before attempting to cross. By this means I kept the Alligators and wild cats at a distance as they can't bear the smell of this crittur. One day I shot at a flock of wild geese as they were sitting on the river and killed three. I quickly stripped and dove in after them; and succeeded in bringing them all safe ashore. But upon looking off on the river I saw a wing broken one. I dove in after it, but it led me such a chase as I never did see before. And just as I was on the point of catching it, I heard a loud howl behind me, that so started me that I jumped right out of water like a sturgeon. I knew it was a bear, and on turning to see how near he was, I saw a wolf but a short distance making towards me. How to get rid of these critturs was the next thing. I div down in a slantindicular direction so as to come up beyond them. When under water an amphibious river calf saw me, and chased me to the surface. Upon breaking water they all began to chase me; luckily there was a planter a few rods distance. I made towards it, and grasping one arm round it caught up a stick of drift wood and prepared to defend myself; upon the wolf's coming within reach, with a good blow over the nose he went off howling. The bear came on, in the most rageriferious manner, so that I was obliged to dodge round the planter, but I gave him some startling raps, when luckily a steam boat seeing this strange sight bore down upon us and just before they reached me the engineer put a rifle ball through the bear's head, and one of the boatmen speared the wolf with a boat hook. And I stunned the River Calf with a blow of my club, so that was taken. I was invited on board, but as there was ladies on board I did not like to appear in a state of natur, so I dove under the boat and swam ashore.

In another issue of the *Almanac*, an equally humorous episode tells of Crockett's difficult fight with a giant Mississippi River catfish.

I cut out one morning to go over the Mississippi on business that concerns nobody but myself. I shoved off my canoe and had paddled into the middle of the stream, when a monstratious great Cat-Fish, better known by the name of a Mississippi Lawyer, came swimming along close under the bows of my boat. I tied a rope around my middle, at one end of it was a fishing spear, and I soon got a chance to dart it into the varmint. He run. and I hauled, and it whirled my canoe round and round like a car-wheel on a railroad. I concluded to stand up to my rack, and I couldn't very well help it, seeing that one end of the rope was made fast to my middle. At last on account of his giving one end of the line a tremendous kick with his tail, and partly on account of the canoe slipping away from under me, I went souse into the water. The cat-fish at the same time seized the slack of my breeches with his teeth and tore them clear off me. I didn't care much for that, as it was easier swimming without them. So I drew out my knife, and when the fish came up and made a pass at my throat with his open mouth, I stabbed out one of his eyes. That made him plunge, but as he was going down I grabbed him by the tail, and went down with him till I touched bottom with one foot. All this time the spear remained in the plaguy varmint, and while under water, I come across a sawyer that was sticking up; I took a turn with my line around this sawyer, and the fish was brought up all standing. So he come at me again, and I manoeuvred to get on the blind side of him—but he could see better under water than I could, though he had but one eye left, and he turned short upon me just as I was about stabbing him to the heart. I then clinched right round his body, and rammed one arm down his throat, while I tried to stab him with the other hand—then I tell you the fire flew. I never see a fellow kick, bite and scratch as he did. I had been under water a pretty good long while, and there was a ringing in my ears that warned me to finish my job as soon as I could. "I tell you there's no quarter to be given," said I to the fish, perceiving him to grow a little faintish. With that he fell to fighting again, and I believe he would have scratched my bones bare, if I had not got a chance to shove my knife to the hilt in his belly. I then cut my line, and rose to the surface pretty well fagged out. Arter I had rested a spell, I dove down and tied a line to the fish and hauled up his corpse. It measured twelve feet in length.

NAUVOO AND THE MORMONS

- 1839 -

It had been a lengthy and twisted road that had carried Joseph Smith to the tiny town of Commerce, Illinois, that long-ago day in 1839. Perched on a bluff overlooking the Mississippi River, the village looked across the "Father of Waters" to Iowa. Just a few miles downstream was Missouri, from whence Smith and his followers had only recently fled.

Smith had founded the Church of Jesus Christ of Latter-day Saints, more commonly called the Mormon Church, nine years earlier in Seneca County, New York, his home at the time. The sect now claimed several hundred followers. Smith claimed that as a youth he had been visited by a "pillar of light above the brightness of the sun at noon day," and that "the Lord opened the heavens upon me, and I saw the Lord and he spake unto me saying, 'Joseph my son, thy sins are forgiven thee. Go thy way, walk in my statutes, and keep my commandments.'" Sometime later, according to Smith, an angel visited him and revealed the location of some golden plates, which he was instructed to eventually interpret and publish. The result was the *Book of Mormon,* released one month before Smith organized the church.

About one year after Smith established the Church, he and his fledgling congregation moved to Kirtland Mills, in Ohio's Western Reserve. Although Kirtland was recognized as headquarters for the Mormons, more and more of the congregation migrated across the Mississippi River and settled in Jackson County, Missouri. It took only a brief time for the older residents of Missouri and the newly arrived Mormons to have a falling-out. Most Missourians were originally from the South and embraced a pro-slavery philosophy. The liberal, northern Mormons frowned on this attitude and were anti-slavery. Additionally, the Mormons considered Missouri to have been bestowed upon them as a kind of divine gift, and their logic about this issue failed to gain many friends. In 1833, after a particularly terse anti-slavery article appeared in the local Mormon newspaper, the old-timers forcibly expelled their neighbors from Jackson County.

While the Missouri Mormons relocated to nearby counties in the state, affairs at Kirtland were improving. Smith, who had not made the trip to Missouri, built a monumental temple and the congregation continued to grow. But, in 1837, after the bank he had founded failed in the recent financial panic, Smith pulled up stakes and moved to the far side of the Mississippi.

In the new locales in Missouri, history repeated itself for the Mormons. Older residents resented the newcomers and their faith that, by now, was rumored to embrace polygamy. General disorder followed, and something close to rebellion caused the death of many people on both sides. The Mormons organized their own militia to protect themselves, while the governor called out the state militia with instructions to run the religious zealots out of

Missouri once and for all. Again, several thousand Mormons were on the run, this time, back across the broad Mississippi River to Illinois.

Joseph Smith was about six months late in arriving in Illinois. He had been arrested and imprisoned by Missouri authorities and charged with treason. When he was finally released, he followed his ousted congregation to the town of Commerce, located a few miles north of Quincy. Smith liked what he saw, negotiated for the purchase of a large tract of land, renamed the small village Nauvoo—a Hebrew word meaning "beautiful"—and commenced to rebuild his Mormon kingdom.

Nauvoo grew rapidly. Within five years, the population had exploded to nearly ten thousand souls and Smith had become mayor of the predominantly Mormon town. A great temple was begun that would serve as the focus of the sect's civic and religious life. For a while, it seemed that Smith's enigmatic "promised land" had finally been found, and that this place might serve as the center of Mormon activities in America.

But, just as rapidly as acceptance by western Illinois residents was extended to the Mormons, it was taken away. Additionally, by now, there was major dissension among the Mormons themselves, the primary issue being the importance that polygamy held within the Church. Again, stories circulated that, in fact, Smith and his closest lieutenants had embraced the practice, while others denied the charge. When, in 1844, a rival Mormon newspaper printed an "expose" of Smith and his alleged polygamous beliefs, Smith ordered the paper destroyed. Along with his brother, Hyrum, he was promptly arrested, charged with a number of criminal acts, and imprisoned in the jail at nearby Carthage. Almost providentially, Smith foresaw that he would not survive this ordeal. On June 24 he wrote:

*I am going like a lamb to the slaughter; but I am calm
as a summer's morning; I have a conscience void of
offense towards God, and towards all men. I shall die
innocent, and it shall yet be said of me—he was mur-
dered in cold blood.*

Three days later, while the Smith brothers were awaiting trial, a
mob of angry townspeople forced its way past guards at the jailhouse
and killed them both.

Just as providentially, Smith, some four months before his murder, foresaw that the rapidly developing hostilities at Nauvoo could
not last much longer. He wrote in his diary that he was investigating
locations in California and Oregon:

*where we can remove to after the temple is completed,
and where we can build a city in a day, and have a
government of our own, get up into the mountains,
where the devil cannot dig us out, and live in a health-
ful climate, where we can live as old as we have a
mind to.*

Soon after Smith's death, as he had anticipated, Nauvoo's corporate charter was revoked, and members of the Mormon Church
were ordered by Illinois authorities to abandon their property and to
vacate the city.

The Mormon banner was picked up by Brigham Young, who
pushed hard to complete the temple at Nauvoo. As pressure from the
surrounding populace and Illinois authorities increased, however, he
was forced to flee the town. In February 1846, under Young's leader-
ship, close to sixteen thousand Mormons exited Nauvoo, crossed the

Mississippi River once again, and established a temporary camp at Winter Quarters, Nebraska. From there, the emigrant party eventually made it to the Great Salt Lake, where the Mormons established another city that would become their international headquarters.

The fate of Nauvoo and its few remaining residents was not a pleasant one. Illinois ruffians forced the last of the Mormons to flee in terror, while the beloved temple was desecrated and burned. A few months after the mass exodus from the city, an observer commented that its "gloomy streets bring a most melancholy disappointment." In time, French Icarians settled the town and briefly experimented with a communal form of government, which, like the previous Mormon attempts, eventually failed.

GENERAL ULYSSES GRANT'S
FIRST VICTORY

- 1861 -

Although President Ulysses S. Grant's two-term administration (1869–1877) was plagued by inefficiency, graft, and corruption, the former highest-ranking general in the Union army still maintains his position as one of America's greatest heroes. And, of all the U.S. presidents, Grant, as much or more than any of the others, was associated with the Mississippi River valley throughout much of his life.

Born Hiram Ulysses Grant in Ohio in 1822, the young son of a leather merchant was locally educated and, in 1839, was appointed to the United States Military Academy. After graduating twenty-first out of a class of thirty-nine, young Grant—now called Ulysses S. because of an error in his army registration records—traveled to St. Louis to accept his first assignment as brevet-second-lieutenant in the U.S. 4th Infantry stationed at Jefferson Barracks.

Two years later, Grant, now a full second-lieutenant, was shipped off to Texas to serve with General Zachary Taylor during the last days before war was declared with Mexico. When hostilities finally began, Grant served with distinction in the battles at Palo Alto, Reseca de la Palma, Monterey, Vera Cruz, Cerro Gordo, and Chapultepec. A few days after he and the rest of the American army entered Mexico City, he was promoted to first-lieutenant.

Shortly after the Mexican War ended, Lieutenant Grant returned to St. Louis where he soon married Julia Dent. In 1854, after serving in military posts in New York, Michigan, California, and Oregon, he resigned his captain's commission in the army and took up the farmer's life near St. Louis.

During the next six years, Grant worked alternatively as a farmer, a firewood merchant, and a real estate agent. Finally, not all too happy with any of these occupations, he moved across the Mississippi River and settled in Galena, Illinois, where he began working with his brothers in his father's hardware and leather store. In April, 1861, when the news of Fort Sumter's Confederate takeover reached Galena, former captain Grant joined the Illinois adjutant-general's staff and was placed in charge of recruiting volunteers. By the summer of 1861, Grant had been promoted to brigadier-general of volunteers and sent to Missouri where he took command of a large military district consisting of the southern portions of Missouri and Illinois.

Grant immediately occupied Paducah, Kentucky, thus preventing the Confederate army from getting there first. Then, during the early days of November, 1861, he led a tiny flotilla, accompanied by about three thousand soldiers, down the Mississippi River and met his Confederate foe, Major-General Leonidas Polk, head to head at the country village of Belmont, Missouri. His first taste of battle as a general officer in the tragic war that pitted American against American served as a proving ground for the ambitious Grant and provided him with a great deal of practical, high-level command experience that would serve him well in the months to come.

After early Union embarrassments at Bull Run, Virginia, and Wilson's Creek, Missouri, President Abraham Lincoln was delighted to see the thirty-nine-year-old Grant showing such aggressiveness and valor in attacking a superior Confederate army. So far, Lincoln's generals had shown little stomach for battle and had provided him with only flimsy excuses for their failures. It was, indeed, a joy to receive news that a former hardware merchant from his home state of Illinois had the courage to resist the enemy, whereas his professionally trained military corps did not.

Although the battle at Belmont served as a springboard to catapult Grant into the national spotlight, it accomplished little as far as the bigger picture of the War was concerned. Belmont was located across the Mississippi River from a well-fortified Confederate position at Columbus, Kentucky. The Union surprise left the small hamlet temporarily occupied by Grant and his small army, but General Polk's men retook the region quickly. More than twelve hundred casualties were suffered—divided about equally between Grant's and Polk's command—in the brief encounter.

After the battle, the question of prisoner exchange came up. During the early days of the War, affairs on the battlefield were far more casual than they ultimately became. Accordingly, General Grant and Confederate brigadier-general Benjamin Franklin Cheatham held a conference whose theme quickly turned from the welfare of prisoners to horse racing. Grant, the leading equestrian in his class at West Point, and Cheatham, the grandson of one of Nashville's founders and a lover of fine horses, soon found themselves joking that perhaps the two opposing sides should simply have a horse race to decide the fate of the prisoners.

General Grant's next big challenge also took place in the Mississippi River valley. In late January 1862, he reported to his superiors in St. Louis that if he were given permission, he would like to march on the Confederate Fort Henry, strategically located along the Tennessee River a few miles northwest of Nashville. Fort Henry and its sister post, Fort Donelson, built nearby on the Cumberland River, were strongly fortified with men and matériel, and the two fortresses together protected Nashville from the north. Permission was approved and Grant began implementing his campaign in early February.

A Union flotilla had already threatened the Confederate garrison at Fort Henry, so by the time Grant and his fifteen-thousand-man army arrived there on February 6, the fort had already surrendered. When it became clear that the Confederate command intended to defend the larger, more formidable Fort Donelson, Grant moved his men across the narrow spit of land that separated the Tennessee River from the Cumberland and prepared to attack.

Union gunboats and ironclads commenced attacking Fort Donelson on the morning of February 14. The following day proved to be a difficult one with fighting continuing during the daylight hours and resulting in a near-victory for the Confederates. But the opportunity was not seized, and the next morning, Brigadier-General Simon Bolivar Buckner, the Confederate officer left behind to handle the surrender, sent a message to General Grant asking for terms of surrender. Grant's reply was short but to the point:

> *Yours of this date, proposing an armistice and appointment of Commissioners to settle terms of capitulation, is just received. No terms except unconditional and immediate surrender can be accepted. I propose to move immediately upon your works.*

From that point on, Grant's initials, "U. S." came to stand for "Unconditional Surrender."

Grant's tenacity, bolstered by several bad decisions made on the part of the Confederate command at Fort Donelson, resulted in the fall of the fort and made possible the occupation of Nashville, the first large Southern city to succumb to Union forces. And, Grant's escapades in the Mississippi River valley would soon make national news again, first from the bloody battlefields at Shiloh and, later, from Vicksburg, the Confederate "Gibraltar of the West."

THE GREAT SIOUX UPRISING

- 1862 -

By the summer of 1862, residents of the Santee Sioux villages situated along the middle Minnesota River, a tributary of the Mississippi, were weary of the constant influx of German settlers in the area and frustrated from seeing their government annuity payments stolen by unscrupulous traders. On August 17, when four young Santee tribesmen killed five German farmers, the uneasy peace that had existed between the Sioux and the settlers rapidly deteriorated.

New Ulm, the primary village in the region, had been settled by a German emigration society in 1854. Over the past eight years, the community had grown in population to more than seven hundred, and the German farmers and their Scandinavian neighbors felt they had done well by migrating to this remote part of frontier Minnesota.

Little Crow, a leader of the Sioux peace faction, had always tried to maintain friendly relations with the whites, but after much cajoling by the more war-like elements in his tribe, he was persuaded to take up the tomahawk against the European farmers in the area. On the following day, four hundred German and Scandinavian settlers were killed by a large body of Sioux warriors. A few days later, Little Crow, with a force of eight hundred men, attacked Fort Ridgely. There, the garrison was armed with howitzers, and the blistering artillery fire laid down by the defenders discouraged the Indians and sent them into retreat, causing one brave to remark, "That gun the soldiers used at the end was terrible."

On August 19, Little Crow's warriors attempted to raid the village of New Ulm, but after only desultory fighting, a severe thunderstorm sent the Indians scurrying for cover. Again, on August 23, a Sioux band numbering about 350 braves struck New Ulm. The townspeople put up a brave defense, but in the end, several hundred more settlers were slaughtered.

Jacob Nix was an eyewitness to the entire Sioux uprising of 1862. Nix, a forty-year-old emigrant who had fled the German revolution of 1848 and eventually arrived in New Ulm in 1858, was placed in charge of defending his village as soon as the news reached its citizens that the Santee Sioux were on the warpath. He published his memoirs of the bloody event of 1887 under the title, *The Uprising of the Sioux Indians in Minnesota, 1862.* Among the volume's pages, the following interesting passage vividly describes what Nix observed on the day that New Ulm was attacked.

On the southeast corner of Minnesota and Center Sts. stood a large log house. The front part of this building was a blacksmith shop, the back part was the dwelling of the blacksmith, Mr. August Kiesling. This strong bulwark was located outside of the barricades but was occupied by our men. Suddenly, shortly before 4:30 p.m., the Indians, with terrible cries, attacked with increased manpower and took the blockhouse, the strongest position of the southeast side of the town. Now the moment had arrived which was to determine New Ulm's existence. If, within a quarter of an hour, the Indians could not be driven out of this position which was so advantageous to them and so dangerous to the defenders, then all would be lost, because the center of the town, between the two main barricades on the north side of Minnesota St. was now exposed to the gunfire of the Indians. And they did not hesitate for a moment to maximize the advantage they had gained.

Fortunately, for the residents of New Ulm, sixty to seventy townsmen, under the command of Jacob Nix, came to the rescue and drove the Indians, who had outnumbered the Germans by four to one, from the blockhouse. "The town was saved," wrote Nix, "but how great were the sacrifices."

Among the casualties of the bloody battle at New Ulm was an early victim of American friendly fire. Nix sadly reported the circumstances of the incident in his book.

In the evening, then, the gunfire of the besieged was reduced to only single shots, which were either fired at random, or at any object which in the darkness one mistook for an Indian. In the cool and dark evening the baker of the besieged town, clad in a buffalo coat, was on his way to his bakery on Broadway. He was mistaken for an Indian . . . . The name of this dutiful man, who was tireless in his efforts during the siege of New Ulm, and who so sadly lost his life, was Jacob Castor.

During late summer of 1862, former United States congressman and former Minnesota governor Henry Hastings Sibley was placed in command of the military contingent being organized for punitive action against Little Crow and his followers. Sibley, a one-time fur trader for the American Fur Company, had a deep respect for the Indians and on more than one occasion had championed their cause in the halls of Congress. But, now, things were different. He had been charged with defeating the Santee Sioux, and that is exactly what he and his army did during a heated battle with Little Crow and his warriors at Wood Lake in late September. The Sioux defeat at Wood Lake broke the Indian resistance once and for all. Several hundred white captives were released and in the ensuing weeks, many tribesmen and their families surrendered to Sibley's forces.

After the affair at Wood Lake, Sibley held court for nearly four hundred captured Santee Sioux warriors and sentenced around three hundred of them to death for their participation in the uprising. When the names of the convicted were sent to President Abraham Lincoln for approval, however, he commuted the sentences of 265 men and allowed the death sentence to stand for 38 others. They were hanged at Mankato, a town situated about fifteen miles from New Ulm, on December 26, 1862.

Ironically, neither Little Crow nor the four young men who were responsible for the bloody Sioux uprising were ever captured, nor did they surrender. They fled to Dakota, seeking refuge, but the following year, Little Crow returned to Minnesota where he was killed in a farmer's berry patch. His body was dumped on a trash heap in Hutchinson, Minnesota, where it stayed until someone rescued the skeleton, which eventually became the property of the Minnesota Historical Society. In 1971, his remains were re-interred in a Sioux cemetery in South Dakota.

THE BATTLE FOR VICKSBURG

- 1863 -

In early July 1863, while the drama of Gettysburg was being played out in the farmlands of southern Pennsylvania, a spectacle of equal intensity was witnessed by the residents of the small, sleepy town of Vicksburg, Mississippi. Up for grabs was what Union commanders called the "Gibraltar of the West," the last major Southern strongpoint on the Mississippi River and an invaluable base of operations in the Confederacy's Western Theater.

For the past six months, hit and miss skirmishes by both Union and Confederate troops had kept the region's populace on their toes. Gunboat activity up and down the Mississippi between Memphis and Port Hudson had alternatively scored successes for both sides. On April 2, seemingly satisfied that Confederate forces had command of the situation, President Jefferson Davis issued a statement approving General John C. Pemberton's defense of the Vicksburg sector, commenting that:

. . . by his judicious disposition of his forces and skilful selection of the best points of defence [sic] he has repulsed the enemy at Vicksburg, Port Hudson, on the Tallahatchie and at Deer Creek, and has thus far foiled his every attempt to get possession of the Mississippi river and the vast section of country which it controls.

A letter written by Davis to the governor of Arkansas the following day was less convincing. Obviously concerned about possession and control of the Mississippi River, Davis advised that:

If we lost control of the Eastern side, the Western must inevitably fall into the power of the enemy. The defense of the fortified places on the Eastern bank is therefore regarded as the defense of Arkansas quite as much as that of Tennessee, Mississippi, and Louisiana.

The concerns of President Davis were realized on April 16, when United States Acting Rear Admiral David Porter, commanding a flotilla of twelve Union gunboats, barreled down the Mississippi past the heavy Confederate artillery batteries that protected Vicksburg. Porter was on his way downriver to link up with General Ulysses S. Grant and his forty-thousand-man army, now poised on the west bank of the Mississippi, and to provide cover for Grant's bold river crossing below Vicksburg.

A couple of weeks later, Davis received more bad news. Colonel Benjamin H. Grierson and nearly two thousand Union cavalrymen, in an attempt to draw Confederate attention away from Grant's massing of troops below Vicksburg, had left La Grange, Tennessee, on April 17, headed for Baton Rouge, Louisiana. During the sixteen-day ride deep into Southern territory, Grierson's troops traveled six hundred miles, fought in four skirmishes, killed or captured six hundred Confederates, destroyed sixty miles of railroad and telegraph lines, and captured three thousand small arms and one thousand horses and mules. The Confederate high command was stunned.

The Union army's river crossing was made during the first few days in May. When it was complete, a thankful Grant wrote, "All the campaigns, labors, hardships, and exposures, from the month of December previous to this time, that had been made and endured, were for the accomplishment of this one object." He now poised his large army to march inland, northeastward, toward Jackson, Mississippi. After he occupied the state's capital city, he intended to turn due west and march on Vicksburg, striking from the east, the least protected and most difficult to defend approach.

On May 7, President Davis, alarmed by Grant's bold movements toward Jackson, wired General Pemberton, the commander of Mississippi troops. "Am anxiously expecting further information of your active operations," read the telegram. "To hold both Vicksburg and Port Hudson is necessary to our connection with Trans-Mississippi." Two days later, Davis assigned General Joseph E. Johnston the responsibility of the Mississippi theater, but left Pemberton in charge of defending Vicksburg.

In a miserable rainstorm that allowed visibility of only a few yards, General Grant's army marched on Jackson during the morning of May 14. General Johnston, accompanied by only around twelve thousand Confederates, evacuated the city and moved north. The hasty retreat allowed the Union forces to occupy the capital, then turn immediately westward, thereby placing themselves between Johnston and the beleaguered defenders of Vicksburg. Four days later, General Pemberton's weary Southerners looked across the defensive works that protected the town on the east and watched as thousands of Union troops rapidly approached. Johnston ordered Pemberton to evacuate, but it was too late for that. Instead, Pemberton passed down the word to prepare for a long siege.

On May 22, Grant threw his entire forty-five-thousand-man force against the defenses of Vicksburg. Despite several Union advances throughout the day, the Confederates won in the end and repulsed the numerically superior opposing army. Grant's command suffered nearly thirty-two hundred casualties, compared to Pemberton's five hundred. A wiser Ulysses Grant made the decision never to attack Vicksburg again, but rather to wait out the siege and let starvation, thirst, and dwindling supplies take their toll.

For the next six weeks, Vicksburg's forty-six hundred townspeople lived in total isolation from the rest of the world. Grant's army commenced shelling the village with mortar and artillery fire. A resident sarcastically wrote,

> *Twenty-four hours of each day these preachers of the*
> *Union made their touching remarks to the town. All*
> *night long their deadly hail of iron dropped through*
> *roofs and tore up the deserted and denuded streets.*

His sentiments were shared by a Confederate soldier who wrote:

> *One day is like another in a besieged city—all you can*
> *hear is the rattle of the Enemy's guns, with the sharp*
> *crack of the rifles of their sharp-shooters going from*
> *early dawn to dark and then at night the roaring of the*
> *terrible mortars is kept up sometimes all this time.*

As the days of June wore on, Grant was re-supplied with fresh troops, while Vicksburg's townspeople slowly starved to death, many of them forced to eat rats and other vermin. On July 3, the day the Gettysburg campaign ended in faraway Pennsylvania, Generals Pemberton and Grant met outside Vicksburg to discuss surrender terms. Twenty-four hours later, Vicksburg's entire garrison, consisting of some twenty-nine thousand soldiers, turned over their weapons to Grant's troops and exited the town on parole.

THE DESTRUCTION OF THE *SULTANA*

- 1865 -

The month of April, 1865, was an eventful one for Americans, both northern and southern. On the twelfth of the month General Robert E. Lee surrendered his Army of Northern Virginia to General Ulysses S. Grant at Appomattox Court House, Virginia. For all intents and purposes, the War Between the States was over. Then, three days later, President Abraham Lincoln died as a result of an assassin's bullet to the back of his head as he watched a play at Ford's Theatre in Washington, D.C. But, one of the most disastrous, yet little-known, events occurred on April 27, when hundreds of Union army prisoners of war were killed in the middle of the Mississippi River as the steamboat carrying them to freedom exploded.

One of the great tragedies of the War was the prisoner situation that existed on both sides. Before the conflict had run its bloody course, nearly half a million men, both Union and Confederate, had been captured and imprisoned in makeshift facilities. Close to fifty thousand soldiers died of disease and hunger in the filthy, overcrowded POW camps. During the early years of the War, there had been no need for prison facilities, since captives were paroled soon after they were caught and swapped for prisoners on the opposing side on the promise that they would not take up arms again. However, the liberal program had eventually been terminated by General Grant, who had exclaimed, "If a system of exchange liberates all prisoners taken, we will have to fight on until the whole South is exterminated."

Soon after the War ended, the United States government started the business of paroling both sides' prisoners and sending them home. Camp Fisk, near Vicksburg, Mississippi, was designated as the primary exchange point for Union prisoners captured in the Western Theater of operations. Authorities soon determined that one of the fastest and most economical methods of transporting the former prisoners from Camp Fisk back to the North was by utilizing steamboats on the Mississippi River. Consequently, contracts were quickly let and several steamship operators, eager to cash in on the sizable operation which paid ten dollars for each officer's passage and five dollars a head for enlisted men, were hastily hired. By late April 1865, a number of steamers tied up to the dock at Vicksburg and loaded the hordes of Union prisoners who anxiously awaited reunion with their families in the North.

One of the boats hired to transport the prisoners back home was the *Sultana,* a medium-sized side-wheeler. The packet had been built at a cost of $55,000 and had been launched in Cincinnati two years earlier. It measured 260 feet long and displaced more than 700 tons. The boat was designed for a maximum load of thirteen hundred tons of cargo in addition to around four hundred fifty passengers and crew members.

The *Henry Ames* was the first boat to leave Vicksburg, and it carried around thirteen hundred parolees. When it came time for the *Sultana* to load up, hundreds of men, most of them from the Confederate prisons at Andersonville, Georgia, and Cahaba, Alabama, quickly poured onboard, anxious to get underway for the trip upriver. But, by the time all of the happy POWs fought their way up the gangplank, the *Sultana* counted nearly nineteen hundred former prisoners, plus eighty-five crewmen, seventy-five civilian passengers, sixty mules and horses, and two hundred fifty hogsheads of sugar.

The *Sultana* moaned and groaned as she pulled away from the dock at Vicksburg, with literally standing room only on her decks. The boat's owners were gleeful as they quickly estimated the huge profit that was going to be made from the voyage. But, the captain and the crew were not happy at all, and they must have wondered how such an overloaded boat could ever successfully fight the strong currents of the flood-fueled mighty Mississippi.

Seventeen hours were required for the *Sultana* to make the relatively short trip from Vicksburg to Memphis. There, the hogsheads of sugar were unloaded. During the early morning hours of April 27, the craft crossed over to the Arkansas side of the river. There, she took on more coal to feed the hungry boilers that were still being drastically overworked from the excess weight aboard. After the *Sultana* left the coaling station at around 1:00 a.m., the crew continuously shoveled coal just to maintain the boat's minimum speed. In time, the red-hot boilers could stand no more and between 2:00 and 3:00 a.m. on April 27, when the steamboat was just a few miles up the Mississippi River from Memphis, they exploded and ripped the *Sultana* to pieces.

What followed was mass confusion. Hundreds of mangled human bodies were literally hurled from the exploding boat into the dark depths of the Mississippi. Boiling hot water and steam from the boilers killed several prisoners. The wood and metal superstructure of the *Sultana* was pulverized from the violent blast and the resulting fire. Some men and animals, temporarily lucky enough to escape the explosion, were consumed by the intense flames. A few soldiers escaped both the explosion and the fire by blindly jumping into the icy waters of the Mississippi River. But, although they were clear of the boat's wreckage, many survivors found themselves hundreds of yards from either shore and unable to swim to safety through the river's icy waters. As late as May 15, decomposed bodies were still washing ashore all the way back to Memphis and beyond.

United States Customs Service records at Memphis later revealed that a total of 1,547 victims died in the *Sultana* tragedy. The official army figure was only 1,238. The true figure can never be known with precise accuracy, since the loading procedures at Vicksburg were so haphazard that reliable records for those who boarded were not kept.

A board of inquiry later delved into the *Sultana* incident. The army officer in charge of the prisoner transfer was court-martialed and released from service, but his conviction was later overturned and he was honorably discharged. The *Sultana*'s engineer had his license revoked, but he was later exonerated of all blame. The War Department made an official announcement that in future transportation matters where army personnel were involved,

> . . . *the strictest attention should be given to prevent the use of any but perfectly safe transports, under experienced and careful masters . . . . The late calamity to the steamer* Sultana *shows the need of extreme caution . . . in the management of river transportation.*

Much of the nation, the northern part at least, was still in mourning over the death of President Lincoln when the *Sultana* met its fate. Consequently, the mishap received only scant attention in the newspapers of the times. However, as events turned out, more people perished during this horrible tragedy on the Mississippi River than were killed on the *Titanic* some fifty years later.

THE *NATCHEZ* VS. THE *ROBERT E. LEE*

- 1870 -

It was bound to have happened sooner or later. Put two equally strong-willed men, but with opposite personalities, together on the same river, each one of them the proud owner of a top-of-the-line, state-of-the-art steamboat, and before long there will be talk about which craft is the fastest. And, that's exactly what happened in late July 1870, when fifty-four-year-old Captain Tom Leathers, standing well over six feet tall and weighing nearly three hundred pounds, decided to try out his boat, the *Natchez,* against the *Robert E. Lee,* operated by fifty-year-old Captain John Cannon.

By 1870, both men were living legends on the Mississippi River and its tributary system. Both had only recently invested several hundred thousand dollars in their respective steamboat lines, and both bragged that their premier boats, Leathers's *Natchez* and Cannon's *Robert E. Lee,* were just about the finest inland watercraft to be found anywhere in the world.

Outside observers were just as complimentary. A reporter for the *New Albany* [Indiana] *Ledger* wrote in 1866, when the *Robert E. Lee* was launched from the boatyard that:

> *The cabin and outfit of this great southern steamer*
> *surpasses that of any boat that ever graced the trade,*
> *and her accommodations are on the same scale of gran-*
> *deur and magnificence . . . . The cabin with its rich*
> *garniture and splendid furniture, dazzling chandeliers,*
> *arched and fretted ceilings etched with gold, stained*
> *glass skylights, immense mirrors, the velvet carpets, the*
> *pure zinc white of the sides, the rosewood stateroom*
> *doors, the imitation Egyptian marble sills, all com-*
> *bined, make it bear an appearance of oriental luxury,*
> *magnificence and splendor seldom conceived and never*
> *before seen floating the cold waters of this so-called*
> *semi-barbarian Western world.*

The *Robert E. Lee* measured three hundred feet long with a beam of forty-four feet, seven feet shorter but one foot wider than the equally, sumptuously equipped *Natchez*. Each boat was powered by two coal-burning engines, one for each of the boat's two side paddlewheels.

Captain Leathers made the low-key challenge for a race between the two boats when he advertised that the *Natchez* would leave New Orleans for its weekly trip to St. Louis on Thursday, June 30, 1870, rather than on Saturday, the normal departure day. Leathers knew that Cannon's *Robert E. Lee,* which plied the lower Mississippi River as well, always left New Orleans on Thursdays. Thus, by announcing that his boat would depart the Crescent City on Thursday, Leathers backhandedly issued the dare to his competitor.

Captain Cannon, aboard the *Robert E. Lee,* was plying down the Ohio River when he heard of Leathers's challenge. Actually, although never one to back down from a wager or a fight, Cannon had second thoughts about conducting a race between his boat and the newer, supposedly faster, *Natchez.* But, on his way down the Mississippi to New Orleans, he made necessary repairs to his boat, anticipating that he would, indeed, accept the challenge.

Both captains advertised in the *New Orleans Picayune* that rumors about a race between the two boats were false, Leathers declaring that "Being satisfied that the steamer *Natchez* has a reputation of being fast, I take this method of informing the public that the reports of the *Natchez* leaving here next Thursday . . . intending racing, are not true." Cannon's response came as no surprise. It read, "Reports having been circulated that steamer *R. E. Lee,* leaving for Louisville on the 30th June, is going out for a race, such reports are not true . . . . "

The rivermen, citizens of New Orleans, the gamblers, and the speculators weren't fooled by the two captains' mild denial of a race. Within days, news of the upcoming battle was relayed all around the world, and it is estimated that several million dollars worth of bets were placed on one boat or the other.

By five o'clock on the afternoon of Thursday, July 30, more than ten thousand anxious onlookers crowded the wharves at New Orleans. There, separated by only two berths, were the magnificent *Natchez* and the *Robert E. Lee,* both cleaned and polished to perfection, and with thick, black smoke pouring out of their twin smokestacks. Captain Cannon got the jump on Leathers, when, exactly at five o'clock, he ordered the mooring lines to be cut on the *Lee,* and headed upriver. Leathers, not a little chagrined at being caught napping, cast off in hot pursuit. Before the last view of New Orleans disappeared around a bend of the river, the *Lee* was already one mile, or three and a half minutes, in front of the *Natchez.*

At 1:30 the following morning, the *Lee* passed Baton Rouge, located about 140 miles upriver from New Orleans. Cannon was running six minutes ahead of Leathers. At Natchez, an unhappy brass band that had been assembled to play for a supposed front-running *Natchez,* of course named in the city's honor, refused to perform when its members observed the *Lee* pulling up to the wharf first. By the time Vicksburg was reached by the *Lee,* twenty-four hours and thirty-eight minutes out of New Orleans, Cannon's craft was fourteen minutes ahead of the *Natchez.*

By the afternoon of July 2, the *Lee* had pulled ahead of the *Natchez* by nearly an hour, and by the time Memphis was reached later that night, the gap had widened by a few more minutes. When Captain Cannon and the *Lee* passed Cairo, Illinois, at around six o'clock in the evening of July 3, they were more than three days out of New Orleans and in unfamiliar waters. In addition to working on the lower Mississippi River, Cannon's boats traditionally plied the Ohio River from Louisville to Cairo, but his officers had never piloted craft in the Mississippi between Cairo and St. Louis, a stretch of the river that was totally familiar to Leathers and his crew. Not to worry, Cannon had several freelance pilots waiting for him at Cairo who were well qualified to take the *Lee* all the way to St. Louis.

After both boats loosed themselves from the same sandbar, having lost about the same amount of time, an area of intense fog was entered, limiting visibility to practically zero. Leathers, believing that Cannon would never risk his men and boat in such treacherous weather and unfamiliar waters, commanded the *Natchez* to tie up until the fog cleared. When he ordered "full speed ahead" the following morning, he learned that Cannon and the *Lee* had never stopped and realized that he was soundly defeated.

At 11:35 a.m. on July 4, the *Robert E. Lee* pulled up to the St. Louis wharf amidst the wild cheering and mirth-making of seventy-five thousand spectators, the largest crowd ever assembled in the city. The time for the twelve-hundred-mile run was three days, eighteen hours, and fourteen minutes.

There have been other races in years past between mighty steamboats on the Mississippi River. But, there never was one that caused greater curiosity, generated more interest, and garnered more bets than the legendary race between the *Natchez* and the *Robert E. Lee*.

THE GREAT MEMPHIS
YELLOW FEVER EPIDEMIC

- 1878 -

Neither Andrew Jackson, nor either of the partners in the land speculation scheme that had brought the three men to the Chickasaw Bluffs from Nashville, would have ever dreamed that the city they were about to lay out on the banks of the Mississippi River would in a few short years be the site of one of the worst epidemics ever to hit America. In 1819, Jackson, still basking in glory from his Battle of New Orleans exploits only four years earlier, along with his former law partner, John Overton, and another wartime hero, General James Winchester, had purchased several thousand acres of mosquito-infested western Tennessee swampland from the Chickasaw Indians and were in hopes of encouraging thousands of settlers from the east to come and settle the newly opened land.

The slow-moving streams and marshy river bottoms that punctuated the region should have been warning signs. All three men lived in the gently rolling hills of the Nashville Basin, and standing, stagnant bodies of water were not a common thing to them. But Jackson had spent a lot of time in Louisiana and Florida and was more than familiar with the effects that a hot, humid climate could have on people. Nevertheless, the land was bought cheaply, and with a little hard work and a lot of forbearance, the partners figured it should make suitable farmland for scores of emigrant families.

Within fifteen years after its 1819 founding, Memphis, as the men proudly called their new town, was booming. An 1834 gazetteer was more than laudatory when it described the rapidly growing village in glowing terms:

> *Memphis, a post town in Shelby county, situated on the east bank of Mississippi river, one mile above the site of old Fort Pickering, at one of the Chickasaw Bluffs, below the mouth of Wolf river. This town stands on one of the most noble bluffs on the river, commanding a fine view of the surrounding country, and from its relative position to the Western District [Nashville], and the late Chickasaw Purchase, it must undoubtedly become the emporium of one of the finest agricultural districts in the western country. Already it is a place of considerable business, and is improving faster than any town in the state.*

By the time the War Between the States began in 1861, Memphis was already a well-established cotton market and ranked high in importance among the major ports in the South. In 1878, despite the rigors and economic woes of Reconstruction, the city boasted a population of forty-eight thousand. But like most other American cities of the times, its sanitation facilities were atrocious. Open privies were the rule, and in most cases—especially among the lower income groups that lived along the riverbank—animal carcasses and garbage were disposed of by simply throwing the refuse into the streets. "I've been to Cairo, and there's dirt for you . . . I've been to Cologne where it's pure smell—but they all back down before Memphis," wrote a less-than-impressed visitor.

In the summer of 1878, Memphis health officials received news that a new yellow fever epidemic was raging in the West Indies. The mosquito-spread disease was no stranger to the city, having visited the Mississippi valley several times before. The latest incident had occurred in 1873 and resulted in about five thousand reported fever cases. A 40 percent mortality rate had been experienced during that particular episode.

During these early times before the mechanisms of many diseases were clearly understood, the city's residents were totally ignorant of the origin of the fever. No doubt, few of them realized that it was the same malady that had caused the expulsion of large British and French armies from the West Indies between 1794 and 1802 after huge manpower losses were sustained during the suppression of a slave revolt. In the eight-year period, around thirty-five thousand of Europe's finest soldiers perished, many more from yellow fever than from the hands of the rebelling slaves.

In late July, word quickly spread throughout the lower Mississippi River valley that the dreaded disease had hit New Orleans. By August 9, it had arrived in Grenada, Mississippi, just one hundred miles south of Memphis. The inevitable occurred on August 13, when the first fatality was reported in the Bluff City. Within ten days of the initial death, twenty-five thousand residents had fled Memphis, leaving about twenty thousand behind to take the brunt of the epidemic. A pall of death hovered over the city as scores of black and white alike breathed their last. John M. Keating, the editor of the local newspaper, the *Daily Appeal,* graphically described what life in the inner city had become since the fever struck.

> *At night it was silent as a grave, by day it seemed desolate as the desert. There were hours . . . as if the day of judgment was about to dawn. Not a sound was to be heard; the silence was painfully profound. Death prevailed everywhere . . . . Even the animals felt the oppression and fled from the city. Rats, cats, or dogs were not to be seen.*

The hot, humid days of late August and early September accentuated the misery being suffered by every citizen of Memphis. Doctors and nurses were severely overworked, and many of them came down with the disease themselves. In all, forty-five physicians died of the fever, suffering the same excruciating pain and debilitating symptoms as their patients.

Two months and five days after Mrs. Kate Bionda became the city's first yellow fever casualty, the weather around Memphis turned sufficiently cold for the formation of a frost. With the accompanying cold came a demise of the mosquitoes responsible for the transmission of the disease. Although neither physicians nor lay people of the day understood why cold weather spelled doom to epidemic diseases, they knew that it did, and great joy was shared by all for the break in the heat which lasted till the end of October. By then, all evidence of the dreaded yellow fever had left Memphis, and the city sighed a breath of relief.

When the fatalities were counted, it was revealed that nearly all of the six thousand white residents who remained in the city during the epidemic's peak became infected with the disease, and more than four thousand of them died. The black population was more fortunate. Out of eleven thousand cases reported, around one thousand perished. At one point in September, two hundred people died each and every day. Many senior city and other government officials stayed in town to ride out the storm, and practically all of them became infected; ironically, only the chief health officer succumbed to the malady. The local undertaker hired on 130 extra employees who were kept busy making coffins and burying the dead. Within a six-week span, they had interred twenty-five hundred bodies.

Although the cold weather brought a temporary end to the great yellow fever epidemic that had struck the entire lower Mississippi River valley in 1878, the disease revisited Memphis the following year. Fortunately, its effects were not as severe as before. Some two thousand cases were reported with 583 fatalities. Subsequent epidemics throughout the valley in 1888, 1897, and 1898, for some reason, left Memphis untouched. By 1905, yellow fever had been conquered, and the once deadly disease was a thing of the past in the United States.

MARK TWAIN AND
THE MISSISSIPPI RIVER

- 1883 -

The single name most frequently associated with the Mississippi River is arguably that of Samuel Langhorne Clemens, better known to the literary world as Mark Twain. Born in 1835 in the frontier village of Florida, Missouri, Clemens spent much of his youth along the mighty Mississippi in the small town of Hannibal, Missouri, located about one hundred river miles upstream from St. Louis. At the age of eighteen, Clemens traveled to New York and Philadelphia where he worked as an itinerant printer's helper. Afterward, he apprenticed himself to a Mississippi River steamship pilot, learned the trade, and followed his new calling until the outbreak of the War Between the States in 1861.

Clemens's next job was with the Confederacy as an officer of Missouri volunteers. In his *Autobiography,* he humorously described his short-lived career in the Southern army.

I was in New Orleans when Louisiana went out of the Union, January 26, 1861, and I started North the next day. Every day on the trip a blockade was closed by the boat, and the batteries at Jefferson Barracks (below St. Louis) fired two shots through the chimneys the last night of the voyage. In June I joined the Confederates in Ralls County, Missouri, as a second lieutenant under General Tom Harris and came near having the distinction of being captured by Colonel Ulysses S. Grant. I resigned after two weeks' service in the field, explaining that I was "incapacitated by fatigue" through persistent retreating.

In the meantime, Clemens's brother, Orion, who was a practicing attorney, had received a federal appointment as secretary for the newly created Territory of Nevada. With eight hundred dollars in silver coin and a huge unabridged dictionary between them, the two brothers hopped the overland stage and headed for Virginia City. Here in the wilds of the American West, Clemens decided to become a journalist for the local *Virginia City Enterprise*. And, he adopted the name, Mark Twain, which would stick with him for the rest of his life. Clemens explained how he picked his *nom de plume* in his *Autobiography*.

At first I roamed around the country seeking silver, but at the end of '62 or the beginning of '63 when I came up from Aurora to begin a journalistic life . . . I was presently sent down to Carson City to report the legislative session. I wrote a weekly letter to the paper;

it appeared Sundays, and on Mondays the legislative
proceedings were obstructed by the complaints of mem-
bers as a result. They rose to questions of privilege and
answered the criticisms of the correspondent with bit-
terness, customarily describing him with elaborate and
uncomplimentary phrases, for lack of a briefer way.
To save their time, I presently began to sign the letters,
using the Mississippi leadman's call, "Mark Twain"
(two fathoms—twelve feet) for this purpose.

After his Virginia City newspaper experience, Clemens, now writing under the name Mark Twain, moved to San Francisco. There, he made friends with Bret Harte, who at the time was working for the U.S. Mint, but who soon would find international fame with the publication of his short story, "The Luck of Roaring Camp." In the meantime, Twain continued to write and, in 1865, produced a short story entitled "The Jumping Frog" in an obscure New York literary journal called *The Saturday Press.* The story was picked up by newspapers all over the country and Mark Twain became an overnight success. Later, the story was published in Twain's first book, *The Celebrated Jumping Frog of Calaveras County, and other Sketches.*

Following a brief tour of the Hawaiian Islands, Twain returned to California and embarked on the lecture tour. Finding mixed success with this medium, he then set off on an around-the-world tour. When he returned to the United States, he wrote of his travels in *The Innocents Abroad,* a huge, two-hundred-thousand-word book. He averaged writing more than three thousand words a day for sixty straight days and completed the manuscript in record time, dryly commenting that such a speed was "nothing for Sir Walter Scott, nothing for Louis Stevenson, nothing for plenty of other people, but quite handsome for me."

In 1870, Twain, now financially secure by the success of *The Innocents Abroad,* married Olivia Langdon. He spent the next couple of years in Buffalo, New York, and in Hartford, Connecticut, pursuing his journalistic career. When the failure of a publishing house in which he had invested placed a heavy financial burden on him, he once again turned to writing books for a living. Between 1872, when he published *Roughing It,* and 1894—a period of twenty-two years—Twain wrote *The Gilded Age,* his first novel and co-written with Charles Dudley Warner; *Old Times on the Mississippi; The Adventures of Tom Sawyer; A Tramp Abroad; Life on the Mississippi; The Adventures of Huckleberry Finn; A Connecticut Yankee in King Arthur's Court;* and *The Tragedy of Pudd'nhead Wilson,* all of which were commercial successes.

Mark Twain's love and respect for the Mississippi River becomes obvious when one realizes how many of his books and short stories gravitate around some aspect of the mighty stream. Many of his books' characters were based on real people he knew while growing up in Hannibal and on his uncle's nearby farm. His desire to be a river pilot was best expressed in his book, *Life on the Mississippi.* In that volume, Twain wrote:

> *When I was a boy, there was but one permanent ambition among my comrades in our village on the west bank of the Mississippi River. That was, to be a steamboatman. We had transient ambitions of other sorts, but they were only transient. When a circus came and went, it left us all burning to become clowns; the first negro minstrel show that ever came to our section left*

us all suffering to try that kind of life; now and then we had a hope that, if we lived and were good, God would permit us to be pirates. These ambitions faded out, each in its turn; but the ambition to be a steam-boatman always remained.

When Mark Twain died in Connecticut in 1910, he was one of America's leading literary voices. His stories of Tom Sawyer and Huckleberry Finn have kept millions of boys all over the world glued to the edges of their seats waiting to read the next scrape that the rowdies would get into. Ernest Hemingway once said that *The Adventures of Huckleberry Finn* was the book from which all other American literature was derived. Today, despite efforts by some politically correct historians and muses, his popularity appears to be at an all-time high.

THE GREAT MISSISSIPPI RIVER FLOOD

- 1927 -

Readers of the April 25, 1927, issue of *Time* were greeted with more of the same succinct reporting that had made the magazine one of the most popular purveyors of news in the United States. They read that Herbert Hoover, then secretary of commerce, had voiced his opinion that the president's cabinet was already too large, and that a newly created post of secretary of education was certainly not needed. If the reader was sports-minded, he might have read with interest that the secretary of war's son, Dwight Davis, Jr., had just been assigned the position of first baseman on Harvard University's baseball team. And, if the weather interested him, he might have been surprised to learn that the entire southern Mississippi River valley, from the mouth of the Ohio River all the way to New Orleans, had been hit by a devastating flood.

An article in the following week's issue was more graphic in its description of the rapidly rising floodwaters. It read:

*Skim ten to twenty-eight feet of water off the surface of
Lake Ontario. Pour it into the Mississippi River basin
from Cairo, Ill., to the Gulf. The resultant swamp will
be a mild picture of the conditions which Spring-
swollen rivers actually produced in the lower
Mississippi valley last week.*

Probably not realized by most readers of the tragic events along
the lower Mississippi was the fact that the woes being unleashed
upon the vast region had their origins almost a year earlier when
heavy rains visited many of the midwestern and prairie states. The
rains continued into the winter and following spring, so that by
April, most tributaries of the Mississippi were swollen to the brim
with water that had no place to go.

On April 21, a large dike near Greenville, Mississippi, burst,
spewing more than two million acres of floodwaters across the surrounding countryside. Later the same day, a similar incident occurred
near Pendleton, Arkansas, sending a wall of water toward the scores
of tiny communities downstream. Twelve miles east of Little Rock,
three families were warned by their neighbors to leave their farms
while there was still time. All three refused. The next morning, flood
waters had inundated by many feet all three farmhouses and everyone in them.

The May 9 issue of *Time* carried the story that Louisiana's governor had ordered a huge levee downstream from New Orleans to be
purposely destroyed, explaining that "Engineers believed that water
drained through the . . . cut would lower the Mississippi flood crest
two to three feet, so that levees protecting New Orleans would not
give way when highwater reached the city." But there were casualties
to the plan. The residents of St. Bernard and Plaquemine Parishes,

located downstream from the destroyed levee, watched as millions upon millions of gallons of silt-laden floodwaters poured across their farms and communities.

By early May, angry Mississippi floodwaters were inching toward the Gulf of Mexico at the rate of one mile per hour. "The crest of the Mississippi flood last week spread through Arkansas and Louisiana the desolation that last fortnight it had brought to Kentucky and Tennessee," declared a *Time* reporter in the May 9 issue. In the wake of the cries of three hundred thousand homeless Southerners, crippled by the submersion of more than six million acres of their choice farmland, President Calvin Coolidge appointed Secretary of Commerce Herbert Hoover to head up the relief effort. The American Red Cross donated $5 million to the cause. In the meantime, disease, contaminated water supplies, and food shortages fueled the already terrible crisis that plagued Mississippi River valley dwellers.

Americans everywhere were comparing the great flood of 1927 with other catastrophes they had experienced or had heard about. The truth was, however, there simply was no comparison. Herbert Hoover exclaimed,

> *There was never in our history such a calamity as this flood, which before it ends will have, I fear, involved more than half a million of our people, creating a problem of relief and rehabilitation, the magnitude of which it is scarcely possible to exaggerate. I sometimes wonder if the people of our country realize just what this calamity is. Do they know that before the flood recedes more than half a million Americans, men, women and children, will have seen their homes swal-*

lowed up in the deluge, their crops destroyed, their
businesses ruined?

Frank Kent, a reporter for the *Baltimore Sun,* declared that
"The San Francisco earthquake and fire does not compare with
this national calamity. Nothing else . . . since the Civil War is in its
class."

By early June, the number of flood-stricken victims had jumped
to 560,000, ranging from 4,200 in Illinois to more than 200,000 in
Mississippi. The Red Cross relief fund had grown to $14 million.
So far, official figures showed that one hundred and fourteen lives
had been lost throughout the lower valley: Arkansas with fifty-nine,
Mississippi with forty-two, Louisiana with nine, Tennessee and
Illinois with two each. More realistically, however, perhaps as many
as five hundred individuals had already died as a direct result of the
flooding.

The June 20 issue of *Time* announced an uneasy truce with the
great Mississippi River flood of 1927. Its journalist wrote that with
the mighty stream's floodwaters "quietly seeping into the Gulf of
Mexico, attention turned toward preventing the river from ever again
driving valley-dwellers from their homes in hundreds of thousands."
An elaborate plan, combining selected reforestation, reservoir and
spillway construction, basin containment, and vital levee placement,
was proposed to prevent a recurrence of such a catastrophe.

But, in the very same issue of *Time,* another small news item
tucked away on page eight must have instilled fear in many a reader.
It reported briefly that:

Meanwhile in Arkansas, Illinois, and Missouri a new
flood was driving valley-dwellers away from the homes
to which they had returned with the receding of the

flood waters which now are running into the Gulf of Mexico.

When the rainy season was finally over, the Mississippi River valley had never before witnessed such a disastrous spectacle as the Great Flood of 1927. Thanks primarily to modern-day flood control techniques, it will probably never see one of such proportions again, the deluges of 1993 and 2008 notwithstanding.

THE STORY OF THE *DELTA QUEEN*

- 1995 -

Years ago, in his book, *Life on the Mississippi,* the American humorist and popular sage, Mark Twain, wrote:

> *She was as clean and dainty as a drawing-room; when*
> *I looked down her long, gilded saloon, it was like gaz-*
> *ing through a splendid tunnel; she had an oil-picture*
> *. . . on every stateroom door; she glittered with no*
> *end of prism-fringed chandeliers, the clerk's office was*
> *elegant, the bar was marvelous, and the barkeeper had*
> *been barbered and upholstered at incredible cost.*

Twain's colorful portrait of a Mississippi River steamboat appeared at a time when hundreds of such vessels still operated along the inland waterways of America. For all intents and purposes, though, his vivid look at a steamboat of yesteryear gives a perfect description of today's *Delta Queen,* one of the last surviving steamers to ply the Mississippi River and its tributary system.

Although the *Delta Queen* has attained her real fame on the Mississippi River during the past half century, the craft was built in Stockton, California, between the years 1925 and 1927, at a cost of one million dollars. From 1927 until 1940, the steamer, along with her sister ship, the *Delta King,* operated as overnight excursion boats on the Sacramento River, making the trip between the state capital and San Francisco in eleven hours. The fare for round-trip passage was a whopping three dollars, and a five-course dinner cost seventy-five cents!

In 1940, the United States government leased the *Delta Queen* and the *Delta King* and placed the boats under the command of the navy, whose personnel promptly mounted guns on the wing bridges and painted both boat's superstructures navy gray. After December 7, 1941, the pair was primarily used to transport military personnel wounded at Pearl Harbor from troop carriers harbored in San Francisco Bay to hospitals in the region.

In 1946, after the *Queen* and the *King* had been decommissioned by the navy, they were placed on the auction block. Captain Tom Greene, who owned a Cincinnati steamboat line, was high bidder for the *Queen* and purchased her for just over forty-six thousand dollars. The *King* was sold to an import/export company with headquarters in Siam.

The process of transporting the *Delta Queen* to Cincinnati began on April 19, 1947, when the steamer was towed away from the California coast and steered toward the Panama Canal. Three weeks later, she became the first steamboat ever to pass through the canal. On May 18, after being on the open sea for twenty-nine days and covering nearly fifty-three hundred miles in the process, the *Delta Queen* entered the mouth of the Mississippi River.

During the fall and winter of 1947–48, the *Queen* was docked at Pittsburgh for repairs and renovation. In June 1948, the boat left Cincinnati for its inaugural cruise on the Ohio River. On board was a very proud Captain Tom Greene and his mother, a respected river pilot herself, Captain Mary Greene.

By 1966, the *Delta Queen's* future was in jeopardy. Federal legislation had recently been passed which prohibited wooden boats from transporting more than fifty overnight passengers. A "Save the *Delta Queen*" campaign was immediately started, and its organizers soon secured more than one million signatures on petitions that were sent to Congress to exempt the *Queen* from the law. An initial exemption was granted and has been renewed several times since so that, at this writing, the *Queen* is still exempt.

In the meantime, in 1970, the *Delta Queen* was added to the National Register of Historic Places and one year later contracted with the government to carry the U.S. mail. The ship's owners, having since changed the corporate name from Greene Line Steamers to The Delta Queen Steamboat Company, added a second cruise ship, the $27 million *Mississippi Queen,* to the fleet in 1976.

In 1989, the *Queen's* sister ship, the *Delta King,* underwent a $10 million restoration and was converted into a floating hotel and conference center on the Sacramento, California, waterfront. During the same year, the *Queen* was designated a National Historic Landmark, joining other such American treasures as Mount Vernon and the Statue of Liberty. In 1990, the *Queen* was totally renovated at a cost of nearly $3.5 million.

In 1995, The Delta Queen Steamboat Company placed into service the largest paddlewheeler ever built. It was christened the *American Queen,* and it was produced at a cost of $65 million. Today, the three sister ships, the *Delta Queen,* the *Mississippi Queen,* and the *American Queen* ply the inland waterways of America, bringing back a style of travel that, although once common, has long since disappeared.

The luxurious *Delta Queen* measures 285 feet long by 60 feet at the beam. It is equipped with a single paddlewheel and carries a gross weight of nearly thirty-four hundred tons. The boat's top speed is about ten miles per hour. Accommodations include four passenger decks and eighty-seven staterooms, capable of handling 174 passengers. Eighty-one crew members are required to operate the craft.

The *Delta Queen* carries practically all of her original fixtures. As one observer wrote, the fine appointments include:

> . . . *Tiffany-style stained glass windows, rich hardwood paneling, gleaming brass, the only ironwood floor aboard a steamboat, and the dramatic Grand Staircase, crowned by an elegant crystal chandelier. Her cabins and staterooms continue the theme of old-fashioned elegance, making a* Delta Queen *voyage on the river the equivalent to a stay at a Victorian bed-and-breakfast.*

Truly, a voyage on the *Delta Queen*, regardless of whether it is for two nights or ten, is like taking a journey back in time to a period when life was simple and unhurried. As Mark Twain once wrote:

> *The face of the water, in time, became a wonderful book . . . and it was not a book to be read once and thrown aside, for it had a new story to tell every day . . . . One cannot see too many summer sunrises on the Mississippi . . . . First, there is the eloquence of silence*

*. . . the water is glass-smooth, then a bird pipes up,
another follows, and soon the pipings develop into a
jubilant riot of music.*

A HURRICANE CALLED KATRINA

- 2005 -

There used to be an old New Orleans saying—often spoken by residents half-jokingly, but at other times dead seriously—that someday visitors would be able to tour the city in gondolas. The truth of that statement became horribly apparent at 6:10 a.m. on Monday, August 29, 2005, when Hurricane Katrina roared out of the Gulf of Mexico and made landfall mere miles southeast of the Crescent City.

Spawned two hundred miles southeast of the Bahaman Islands nearly a week earlier on August 23, Katrina was first classified by the National Hurricane Center as a mere tropical depression, the twelfth of the current hurricane season. The following day, however, authorities upgraded the depression to tropical storm status and thirty hours later, they classified it as "Hurricane Katrina." The fury had only borne its name for two hours when it came ashore in Florida near the Miami-Dade/Broward County line, skipped westward across the extreme southern tip of the peninsula, and hustled back out to sea into the eastern Gulf of Mexico.

By noon on Friday, August 26, Katrina had been upgraded to a Category 2 hurricane, then five hours later to a Category 3. During the day, the governors of both Louisiana and Mississippi declared states of emergency, something the federal government did not do (for Louisiana only) until the following day. On Saturday, Louisiana governor Kathleen Blanco issued a "contraflow" directive that prohibited all incoming vehicular traffic along interstate highways and the opening of the incoming lanes to outgoing traffic with the aim of facilitating the evacuation of New Orleans and vicinity. By the late evening, the National Hurricane Center, hoping against all odds that Katrina would continue its due-westward movement into the far reaches of the Gulf, declared that if the storm did turn northward, it would be on a direct path to New Orleans.

At 1:00 a.m. on Sunday, Katrina was advanced to a Category 4 storm, followed six hours later by its final upgrade—to Category 5 status, the highest and most deadly possible rating. Category 5 hurricanes are capable of sustaining winds up to and in excess of 175 miles per hour, and to the horror of everyone monitoring the dangerous situation, it turned north toward the Louisiana coast. Anticipating the worst, the federal government now classified Mississippi and Alabama to be in "states of emergency" and declared Florida a federal disaster area for the heavy damages already sustained there from Katrina three days earlier.

On Sunday afternoon, Katrina weakened somewhat, giving slim hope to folks along the Gulf coast that maybe the storm would not be as ravaging as authorities had predicted. When it did hit land near the town of Buras, Louisiana, on Monday morning, its winds had, in fact, subsided to 145 miles per hour, reducing its severity status to Category 4. Despite the fact that large portions of New Orleans lie up to twenty feet below sea level and that the city is situated in a bowl-shaped depression between the Mississippi River and Lake

Pontchartrain, optimists hoped that the hurricane would not deliver unmanageable quantities of rainfall, thereby allowing the city's 350 miles of levees to restrain the waters of both the river and the lake.

The storm's thirty-mile-wide eye passed over downtown at around 9:00 a.m. and rapidly raced northward to make another land-fall near the Louisiana-Mississippi state line an hour later. For a few brief minutes, it appeared that New Orleans had survived the worst of the storm, but shortly afterwards, reports were issued that levees along both the Industrial and the Seventeenth Street Canals had been breached, allowing millions of gallons of lake water to pour into the lowest-lying areas. Within hours, upward of eight feet of water cov-ered much of the downtown and eastern parts of the city.

In the meantime, ten thousand New Orleans residents had packed into the Superdome, hoping that it would offer them some measure of protection from the devastating storm. However, with little control over who entered the huge sports arena, home of the New Orleans Saints professional football team, authorities soon found themselves combating rumors of murder, rape, and drug with-drawal within the building even as more and more desperate souls poured in. Later in the morning, part of the dome's roof was ripped off, sending further shock waves of fear into those huddled inside. Other events of that day included the closing of eight Gulf Coast petroleum refineries and the issuance of a statement by the American Red Cross that it was "launching the largest mobilization of resources in its history."

Looting on a monumental scale broke out in the downtown area, and people could be seen walking out of department, appli-ance, and hardware stores with everything from giant television sets to expensive power tools. Sometimes it wasn't as it seemed, however. One woman observed several young men exiting a drug store carry-ing sacks full of unidentifiable merchandise, which she immediately assumed to be expensive loot such as cameras and CDs. Several hours later she came upon the same men passing out cold drinks, energy bars, and medical supplies—the real content of the sacks—to a group of disabled, elderly people who were too fragile to be evacuated from their homes.

So far, officials in Washington, D.C., had maintained a strange silence during the ordeal. On the day the storm made landfall, the director of the Federal Emergency Management Agency (FEMA) waited five hours to request from the Department of Homeland Security that a task force be sent to the region, but then gave it an unbelievable forty-eight hours to respond. Next day, while people along the Louisiana, Alabama, and Mississippi coasts were trying to make some sense out of the horrific suffering they were experiencing, President George W. Bush spoke in San Diego, California, to a group celebrating V-J Day (victory over Japan during World War II). Two days after Katrina hit, Bush flew over the Gulf Coast region on his return to the White House from vacationing in Crawford, Texas, and two days after that actually visited the area on the ground. When asked the day before on national television why the federal government was taking so long responding with assistance, the president replied, "I don't think anybody anticipated the breach of the levees."

In fact, many people, over a period of many years, had been concerned about the strength and resiliency of the levee system in New Orleans. Overseen by the United States Army Corps of Engineers, the levees were designed to maximally withstand Category 3 storms, but critics had predicted that it was just a matter of time before a Category 5 hurricane would hit the city and surrounding area. The army had begged for increased funding to strengthen the system, but, in light of budget cuts, the economy, and an "it can't happen here" attitude, the money never came.

And so, four years after the horror of 9/11, the worst man-made tragedy in American history, Katrina, arguably the country's worst natural disaster, visited New Orleans, bringing with it hurricane force winds that reached in the east as far as the Alabama–Florida border and in the west almost to Morgan City, Louisiana. Estimates vary, and true figures may never be known, but the human toll from the storm has reached at least 1,890 dead and missing, 914 from New Orleans alone. Estimates of the financial losses soar into the billions of dollars.

The effects from Katrina are still being felt by tens of thousands of residents who once made their homes along the Gulf shores of Louisiana, Alabama, and Mississippi. Not only were thousands permanently displaced (hundreds who fled to safe harbor in neighboring states refuse to return to their homes), but recovery for those who have returned has been agonizingly slow.

BIBLIOGRAPHY

Prehistoric Metropolis on the Mississippi: Cahokia

Silverberg, Robert. *The Mound Builders.* New York: New York
Graphic Society, 1970.

Thomas, Cyrus. "Report on the Mound Explorations of the Bureau
of Ethnology," in *Twelfth Annual Report of the Bureau of Ethnology.* Washington, D.C.: Government Printing Office, 1894.

The Kensington Stone

Boland, Charles Michael. *They All Discovered America.* New York:
Doubleday & Company, 1961.

Herrmann, Paul. *Conquest By Man.* New York: Harper & Brothers,
1954.

Holand, Hjalmar R. *Norse Discoveries & Explorations in America:
982–1362.* New York: Dover Publications, Inc., 1969.

Early European Exploration on the Mississippi

Lavender, David. *De Soto, Coronado, Cabrillo: Explorers of the
Northern Mystery.* Washington, D.C.: U.S. Department of the
Interior, 1992.

Williams, Samuel Cole. *Early Travels in the Tennessee Country.*
Johnson City, Tenn.: The Watauga Press, 1928.

The Founding of New Orleans

Du Pratz, Antoine Le Page. *The History of Louisiana.* New Orleans: Pelican Press, Inc., 1947.

The Natchez Revolt

Crutchfield, James A. *The Natchez Trace: A Pictorial History.* Nashville: Rutledge Hill Press, 1985.

Du Pratz, Antoine Le Page. *The History of Louisiana.* New Orleans: Pelican Press, Inc., 1947.

Swanton, John R. *Indian Tribes of the Lower Mississippi Valley.* Washington, D.C.: Bureau of American Ethnology, 1911.

LaClède and the Beginnings of St. Louis

Foley, William E. *A History of Missouri. Volume 1, 1673–1820.* Columbia, Mo.: University of Missouri Press, 1971.

LeCompte, Janet. "Auguste Pierre Chouteau," in *The Mountain Men and the Fur Trade of the Far West,* Volume X, edited by LeRoy R. Hafen. Spokane, Wash.: The Arthur H. Clark Company, 2004.

The Fall of Kaskaskia

Palmer, Frederick. *Clark of the Ohio.* New York: Dodd, Mead & Co., 1930.

Spiller, Roger J., ed. *Dictionary of American Military Biography.* Westport, Conn.: Greenwood Press, 1984.

Waller, George M. *The American Revolution in the West.* Chicago: Nelson-Hall, 1976.

Werstein, Irving. *1776 The Adventure of the American Revolution Told With Pictures.* New York: Cooper Square Publishers, Inc., 1976.

Lewis and Clark at Wood River

Jackson, Donald, ed. *Letters of the Lewis and Clark Expedition with Related Documents 1783–1854.* Urbana, Ill.: University of Illinois Press, 1978.

Lavender, David. *The Way to the Western Sea.* New York: Harper & Row, 1988.

Moulton, Gary E. *The Journals of the Lewis and Clark Expedition.* Volume 2. Lincoln: University of Nebraska Press, 1986.

The Transfer of Louisiana

Dillon, Richard. *Meriwether Lewis: A Biography.* New York: Coward-McCann, Inc., 1965.

Lavender, David. *The Way to the Western Sea.* New York: Harper & Row, 1988.

Sprague, Marshall. *So Vast So Beautiful A Land: Louisiana and the Purchase.* Boston: Little, Brown and Company, 1974.

"Kaintucks" on the Mississippi

Crutchfield, James A. *The Natchez Trace: A Pictorial History.* Nashville: Rutledge Hill Press, 1985.

The New Madrid Earthquake

Clifton, Juanita. *Reelfoot and the New Madrid Quake.* Asheville, N.C.: Victor Publishing Company, 1980.

Great Disasters. Pleasantville, N.Y.: The Reader's Digest Association, Inc., 1989.

The First Steamboat on the Mississippi River

Dohan, Mary Helen. *Mr. Roosevelt's Steamboat.* New York: Dodd, Mead & Company, 1981.

Petersen, William J. *Steamboating on the Upper Mississippi.* New York: Dover Publications, Inc., 1995.

The Battle of New Orleans

Crutchfield, James A. *Tennesseans at War.* Nashville: Rutledge Hill Press, 1987.

Fort Snelling and the Beginnings of Minneapolis-St. Paul

Prucha, Francis Paul, ed. *Army Life on the Western Frontier: Selections from the Official Reports Made Between 1826 and 1845 by Colonel George Croghan.* Norman: University of Oklahoma Press, 1958

———. *Broadax and Bayonet: The Role of the United States Army in the Development of the Northwest 1815–1860.* Lincoln: University of Nebraska Press, 1967.

Wayman, Norbury L. *Life on the River: A Pictorial History of the Mississippi, the Missouri, and the Western River System.* New York: Bonanza Books, 1971.

Frances Wright's Vision

Morris, Celia. *Fanny Wright: Rebel in America.* Chicago: University of Illinois Press, 1992.

Parks, Edd Winfield. "Dreamer's Vision: Frances Wright at Nashoba (1825–1830)," in *Tennessee Historical Magazine,* Series II, Volume II, Number 2. Nashville: Tennessee Historical Society, 1932.

Black Hawk's War

Black Hawk. *Life of Black Hawk.* New York: Dover Publications, Inc., 1994.

Utley, Robert M. and Washburn, Wilcomb E. *The American Heritage History of the Indian Wars.* New York: American Heritage Publishing Company, Inc., 1977.

Discovering the Source of the Mississippi River

Petersen, William J. *Steamboating on the Upper Mississippi.* New York: Dover Publications, Inc., 1995.

Sprague, Marshall. *So Vast So Beautiful A Land: Louisiana and the Purchase.* Boston: Little, Brown and Company, 1974.

George Catlin and the Pipestone Quarry

McCracken, Harold. *George Catlin and the Old Frontier.* New York: Bonanza Books, n. d.

Truettner, William H. *The Natural Man Observed: A Study of Catlin's Indian Gallery.* Washington, D.C.: Smithsonian Institution Press, 1979.

Sandweiss, Martha A. *Pictures From an Expedition.* New Haven, Conn.: Yale Center for American Art and Material Culture, 1979.

Davy Crockett's Mississippi River Exploits

Davy Crockett's Almanacks 1835–1843: The Nashville Imprints. Union City, Tenn.: Pioneer Press, 1986.

Nauvoo and the Mormons

Lamar, Howard R., ed. *The New Encyclopedia of the American West.* New Haven, Conn.: Yale University Press, 1998.

General Ulysses Grant's First Victory

Faust, Patricia L., ed. *Historical Times Illustrated Encyclopedia of the Civil War.* New York: Harper & Row, 1986.

Long, E. B. *The Civil War Day by Day: An Almanac 1861–1865.* Garden City, N.Y.: Doubleday & Company, Inc., 1971.

The Great Sioux Uprising

Tolzmann, Don Heinrich, ed. *The Sioux Uprising in Minnesota, 1862: Jacob Nix's Eyewitness History.* Indianapolis: Max Kade German-American Center, Indiana University-Purdue University at Indianapolis, and Indiana German Heritage Society, Inc., 1994.

Utley, Robert M. and Washburn, Wilcomb E. *The American Heritage History of the Indian Wars.* New York: American Heritage Publishing Company, 1977.

The Battle for Vicksburg

Faust, Patricia L., ed. *Historical Times Illustrated Encyclopedia of the Civil War.* New York: Harper & Row, 1986.

Long, E. B. *The Civil War Day by Day: An Almanac 1861–1865.* Garden City, N. Y.: Doubleday & Company, Inc., 1971.

The Destruction of the *Sultana*

Faust, Patricia L., ed. *Historical Times Illustrated Encyclopedia of the Civil War.* New York: Harper & Row, 1986.

Garrison, Webb. *A Treasury of Civil War Tales.* Nashville: Rutledge Hill Press, 1988.

Yager, Wilson M. "The Sultana Disaster." *Tennessee Historical Quarterly.* Volume XXXV, Number 3. Nashville: Tennessee Historical Society, 1976.

The *Natchez* vs. the *Robert E. Lee*

Rudolph, Jack. "Going for the Horns," in *American Heritage.* Volume 31, Number 2, February/March 1980. New York: American Heritage Publishing Company, 1980.

Wellman, Manly Wade. *Fastest on the River: The Great Steamboat Race Between the* Natchez *and the* Robert E. Lee. Whitefish, Mont.: Kessinger Publishing Company, 2007.

The Great Memphis Yellow Fever Epidemic

Crosby, Molly Caldwell. *The American Plague: The Untold Story of Yellow Fever, the Epidemic That Shaped Our History.* New York: Penguin Group, 2006.

Keating, John McLead. *A History of the Yellow Fever: The Yellow Fever Epidemic of 1878 in Memphis, Tennessee.* Whitefish, Mont.: Kessinger Publishing Company, 2007.

Weisberger, Bernard A. "Epidemic," in *American Heritage.* Volume 35, Number 6, October/November 1984. New York: American Heritage Publishing Company, 1984.

Mark Twain and the Mississippi River

Lamar, Howard R., ed. *The Reader's Encyclopedia of the American West.* New York: Harper & Row, 1977.

Neider, Charles, ed. *The Autobiography of Mark Twain.* New York: Harper & Brothers, 1959.

The Great Mississippi River Flood

Barry, John M. *Rising Tide: The Great Mississippi Flood of 1927 and How It Changed America.* New York: Simon & Schuster, 1998.

Time. April 25, 1927; May 2, 1927; May 9, 1927; May 16, 1927; May 23, 1927; May 30, 1927; June 6, 1927; June 13, 1927; June 20, 1927.

The Story of the *Delta Queen*

Garvey, Stan. *King and Queen of the River. The Legendary Paddle-Wheel Steamboats* Delta King *and* Delta Queen. Stoddard, Wis.: Heritage Press, 2002.

Tassin, Myron. *The* Delta Queen: *Last of the Paddlewheel Palaces.* Gretna, La.: Pelican Publishing Company, 1981.

A Hurricane Called Katrina

Brinkley, Douglas. *The Great Deluge: Hurricane Katrina, New Orleans, and the Mississippi Gulf Coast.* New York: HarperCollins, 2006.

Time. September 12, 2005; September 19, 2005.

INDEX

ABOUT THE AUTHOR

James A. Crutchfield is a popular western historian and the author of numerous books, including *It Happened in Texas, It Happened in Washington*, and six other It Happened In titles.

He is the author of forty books dealing with various aspects of American history and has contributed hundreds of articles to newspapers, journals, and national magazines, among them *The Magazine Antiques, Early American Life*, and *The American Cowboy*.

Crutchfield's writing achievements have been recognized with awards from Western Writers of America, the American Association for State and Local History, and the Tennessee Revolutionary Bicentennial Commission. A former board member of the Tennessee Historical Society, he presently sits on the Board of National Scholars for President's Park in Williamsburg, Virginia. He and his wife, Regena, reside in a pre–Civil War home in Tennessee.